MW01592773

Front Lines to Power Lines

By Steve Mitnick
& Rachel Moore

Also by Steve Mitnick

Lines Down
How We Pay, Use, Value Grid Electricity Amid the Storm
2013

Lewis Latimer
The First Hidden Figure
2020

Women Leading Utilities
The Pioneers and Path of Today and Tomorrow
2021

Front Lines to Power Lines

by Steve Mitnick & Rachel Moore

PUBLIC UTILITIES
FORTNIGHTLY
Impact the Debate

Public Utilities Fortnightly
Lines Up, Inc.
Arlington, Virginia

Library of Congress Control Number: 2021950061

Authors: Steve Mitnick & Rachel Moore
Editor: Lori Burkhart
Assistant Editor: Angela Hawkinson
Production: Mike Eacott
Cover Illustration: Paul Kjellander

For information, contact:

Lines Up, Inc.
3033 Wilson Blvd
Suite 700
Arlington, VA 22201

First Printing, November 2021

ISBN 978-1-7360142-4-0

Printed in the United States of America.

This book is dedicated to the

Veterans in Energy organization

and to all military veterans

in the electric, natural gas, and water

utilities industry

The cover painting entitled "Man on the Line" is by Paul Kjellander,
the President of the Idaho Public Utilities Commission
and past President of the National Association
of Regulatory Utility Commissioners,
commonly referred to by its acronym NARUC.

Table of Contents

Table of Interviewees

Name	Branch	Organization
Bailey, Frank	Army	Gulf Coast Electric Cooperative
Bedell, Brook	Army	CPS Energy
Benson, Jeff	Marine Corps	South Central Electric Association
Bolton, Scott	Army	PacifiCorp
Brown, Kelcey	Navy	MidAmerican Energy
Brown, Kersha	Army	Consolidated Edison
Buker, Milt	Army	MidAmerican Energy
Carlson, Brian	Marine Corps	Flint Energies
Carter, Monique	Air Force	Georgia Power
Craven, Chad	Marine Corps	Pee Dee Electric North Carolina
Douglass, Rob	Navy	FirstEnergy (until 2016)
Eccleston, Sophia	Army	Florida Power & Light
Gaddis, Quintin	Air Force	Portland General Electric
Grier, Sean	Army	Duke Energy
Hernandez, Kevin	Navy	ScottMadden

Hui, Ming-wa	Army	Xcel Energy
Ihnen, Jeff	Navy	Michaels Energy
King, Josh	Navy	American Water
Krieger, Bill	Navy, Army	Consumers Energy
Lockhart, Jesse	Navy	Flint Energies
Mitchell, Ramon	Army	Portland General Electric
Ostrowski, DeAnne	Navy	Consolidated Edison
Penn, Miranda	Army	Georgia Power
Pixley, Brandon	Army	CPS Energy
Rentz, Iliana	Army	Florida Power & Light
Rich, Mike	Army	American Water
Rollins, Tom	Army	Florida Power & Light
Roper, Stephanie	Army	Consolidated Edison
Rother, Rick	Navy	Xcel Energy
Simon, Chad	Marine Corps	Sam Houston Electric Cooperative
Tolbert, Joe	Navy	Georgia Power
Vander Plas, Brad	Army	Golden Valley Electric Cooperative
Wheeler, Cassandra	Air Force	Georgia Power
Wild, Ron	Air Force	Rocky Mountain Power
Yarbrough, Noah	Air Force	Rocky Mountain Power

See Index for pages featured

Sponsoring This Book

Rather than for sale, this book is being distributed freely throughout the Public Utilities Fortnightly community due to the generous support of some highly respected organizations of our community. They include the American Public Power Association, Edison Electric Institute, Electric Power Research Institute, Florida Power & Light, National Rural Electric Cooperative Association, Portland General Electric, and Southern Company. These organizations believe as do the authors that our nation's veterans deserve to have their stories told and shared widely. It is the hope of the authors that this book will raise awareness of the tremendous contributions veterans make to our nation, on and off the battlefield. Please see the moving statements by the sponsoring organizations on the following pages.

Moving Statements by the Sponsoring Organizations

I've often pointed out the parallels between electric utility and military service. Both callings draw hardworking and dedicated men and women to essential roles that help protect and sustain our American way of life. Growing up in a military family and dedicating the bulk of my career to the electric utility industry, I have lived in these worlds my entire life—both are mission-driven with failure not an option. *Front Lines to Power Lines* should be celebrated for telling these veterans' stories and highlighting the inextricable connection between our armed forces and the electric utility industry.

—Joy Ditto, President and CEO,
American Public Power Association

George Westinghouse and Lewis Latimer were great pioneers of the electric industry, but that is not all they had in common. Both enlisted in the military as teenagers, and their military service had an undeniably positive effect on the shaping of their lives and their incredible careers.

As a retired Lieutenant in the U.S. Navy, I spent two years as a department head on a destroyer and two as a White House aide to the Secretary of the Navy. Those experiences taught me courage, adaptability, organization, critical thinking, and so much more. I recognize the importance of military service in my own life. It helped make me a better leader, and that path led me to EEI.

I am profoundly proud that EEI and our member companies—America's investor-owned electric companies—are committed to attracting veterans to the energy industry and to helping them thrive in the workplace. Through the Troops to Energy Jobs program, we work to connect our nation's military veterans to rewarding energy careers. The program provides a roadmap for entry into skilled utility and engineering programs.

EEI also is a proud sponsor of Veterans in Energy, a professional society for military veterans who are working in the energy sector. VIE provides transition, retention, and professional development support to the growing population of military veterans who have chosen energy careers.

I commend Steve and Rachel for their work to capture veterans' stories in *Front Lines to Power Lines* and for acknowledging that our industry embraces the leadership qualities that are innate in our country's military veterans. I believe that George Westinghouse and Lewis Latimer would be proud.

—Tom Kuhn, President,
Edison Electric Institute

The dedicated men and women of the armed forces who continue their careers in the power sector deliver immeasurable value to society long after their military service has ended. Many have honed skills that directly apply to the sector, such as the countless veterans who have transitioned from nuclear naval vessels to nuclear plants. Others find new ways to expand on their military training to take on different positions across the industry, from lineworkers to plant operators to various technical roles.

While their finely tuned skills help them succeed in energy, the exceptional leadership cultivated through their military experience is even more valuable. Veterans' relentless approaches to finding real solutions, and working together to overcome seemingly impossible obstacles, are crucial to overcome the range of challenges facing the power sector. Their unique capabilities and unquestionable resolve serve as the foundation of exceptional leadership—invaluable attributes for an industry navigating unprecedented change.

I am proud to count military veterans among EPRI's senior leaders. In this time of transformation and always, all of us at EPRI are privileged to work alongside talented veterans who chose to continue serving the public by transitioning to energy.

—Arshad Mansoor, President and CEO,
Electric Power Research Institute

Florida Power & Light Company serves a state that is home to more than 1.5 million veterans. As we deliver America's best energy value, we have long benefited from recruiting and hiring the brave and selfless men and women who have served our country and protected our freedoms in the armed forces. We're proud to be part of NextEra Energy, which employs more than two thousand veterans, or nearly thirteen percent of our workforce. And we're proud that three FPL team members who are veterans are featured in *Front Lines to Power Lines*. There are many individual stories in this book that together show the unique blend of values, experience, skills, and discipline that veterans bring to our industry, our state, our country, and to society as a whole.

—Eric Silagy, President and CEO,
Florida Power & Light Company

At the National Rural Electric Cooperative Association, we strongly believe that hiring and caring for veterans and military spouses strengthens our cooperatives and our communities. In forty-eight states, the electric cooperative mission is to power communities and empower members to improve the quality of their lives. This enables every co-op employee to perform their duties with a unified sense of purpose.

We're proud to sponsor *Front Lines to Power Lines* and recognize the dedication and selfless commitment of military veterans across the electric industry. As we've seen time and again, leadership experiences position a veteran to transition to electric cooperatives, quickly establish themselves, and help their team perform at the highest levels. Military veterans bring a sense of duty they had during their service careers to maintaining and innovating the energy system that powers their communities.

We celebrate in this book the commitment, leadership, and spirit our military veterans demonstrate in service of forty-two million people who each day depend on America's electric cooperatives.

—Jim Matheson, CEO,
National Rural Electric Cooperative Association

Veterans of all eras, new and old, answered the important call to serve their country. These bravest citizens among us have chosen to be a part of something larger than themselves in the name of our freedom. We are grateful to the men and women in uniform who risk their lives on behalf of our country.

Veterans have long been a part of Portland General Electric's history and its success. From both World Wars to modern day conflicts in Iraq and Afghanistan, we are grateful for their service and proud of their leadership.

Service to our customers, community members and colleagues, as well as mutual assistance to help our peers, defines the utility industry. Our veteran co-workers, from those who served many decades ago, to those who continue to serve on active duty today, are an integral part of our company's leadership and success.

The military instilled in them strong values of selfless service, loyalty, respect, and discipline. We are inspired by the many veterans at Portland General who apply these values and their talents in serving customers every day and accelerating the clean energy transition.

—Maria Pope, President and CEO,
Portland General Electric

Those who serve in the military selflessly volunteer their lives to guarantee that our American freedoms—life, liberty, and the pursuit of happiness—continue unabated. Our veterans—like Georgia Power's Monique Carter, Miranda Penn, Joe Tolbert, and Cassandra Wheeler, whom the authors wonderfully profile in this book—represent the best our country has to offer, and I enjoy every opportunity I get to meet with veterans and share in their stories.

I am so proud that Southern Company continues to be recognized as a great place for veterans to work. Just this month, Southern Company was recognized as the number one company in the entire U.S. on the Military Times Best for Vets Employer list. We are very fortunate to have thousands of veterans be part of our team. Across the Southern Company system, veterans comprise more than ten percent of our workforce.

For years, Southern Company has cultivated a work environment that is welcoming for veterans. We continuously evaluate our recruiting efforts, retention practices, and support programs to ensure we are providing the assistance and flexibility veterans and those in the reserves require.

Further, we provide opportunities for service members to transfer their military skills and training into careers in the energy sector through on-site job training, creating a recruiting pipeline once their service is complete. As a company, we know that lessons regarding discipline, commitment, and leadership service members receive during their enlistment instills in them qualities and values that perfectly align with who we are as a company.

At Southern Company, we have a special responsibility to uphold values such as safety, trust, commitment, and excellence while adhering to ideals such as leadership, teamwork, adaptability, focus, and service as we work on behalf of millions of customers to provide clean, safe, reliable, and affordable energy.

I am a firm believer that you can never say thank you enough in this world, so please make it a point today to find some way to thank a veteran. We all owe each and every one of them an enormous debt of gratitude.

—Tom Fanning, Chairman, President & CEO,
Southern Company

Acknowledgements

The authors would like to thank the incredible folks at Veterans in Energy, including Cassandra Wheeler, John Broschak, Hal Pittman, Jim Spiers, Kelcey Brown, Howard Gartland, Iliana Rentz, Bradley Pellegrin, DeAnne Ostrowski, and Lavonne Rose. Many of these individuals were helpful in connecting us with many of our interviewees, or allowing us to interview them, and helped us gain perspective on the unique position of veterans within the energy and utilities industry.

We also extend our thanks to all the individuals who volunteered to tell their stories and took the time to interview for this book. They are Frank Bailey, Brook Bedell, Jeff Benson, Scott Bolton, Kersha Brown, Milt Buker, Brian Carlson, Monique Carter, Chad Craven, Rob Douglass, Sophia Eccleston, Quintin Gaddis, Sean Grier, Kevin Hernandez, Ming-wa Hui, Jeff Ihnen, Josh King, Bill Krieger, Jesse Lockhart, Ramon Mitchell, Miranda Penn, Brandon Pixley, Mike Rich, Tom Rollins, Stephanie Roper, Rick Rother, Chad Simon, Joe Tolbert, Brad Vander Plas, Ron Wild, and Noah Yarbrough.

Foreword by Rachel Moore

I grew up surrounded by men and women in uniform. When my father had his Army buddies at our house, his party trick was to have me, at six years old, recite the Pledge of Allegiance and sing every patriotic song I knew by heart. At that age, I wanted nothing more than to join the military and follow in his footsteps. Every successful adult I knew was either an active service member or a veteran.

But my father's success was hard won. At nineteen years old, he was living on his own. He had a car that his parents had helped him buy, but it died. He then got his first motorcycle, which his grandfather loaned him money to fix. Sadly, the motorcycle was later stolen.

By the time my father reached twenty-one years old, he was using public transportation and couldn't keep a roof over his head without a roommate. The way he told the story, he joined the Army because he felt that he had no other options. The Army provided a lot of things my father needed to live, like housing, food, and money in general. But the lessons the Army provided in loyalty, duty, respect, service, honor, integrity, and courage were what he really needed at the time.

When my father retired as a Sergeant Major after twenty-six years served, he started a second career as a government contractor. Meanwhile, I was joining the Air Force Junior Reserve Officer Training Corps at my high school. I ended my career at AFJROTC Unit 20012 as a Cadet Second Lieutenant, serving my fellow cadets as a logistics officer. Later, as I was graduating, I was accepted to Virginia Tech as a Corps of Cadets applicant.

Unfortunately, a boxing injury and its resulting nerve problems and muscle atrophy in my hands prevented me from following through on those dreams. To the university's credit, a representative from Virginia Tech insisted that I would still be allowed to join the Corps and live out my college years as a cadet, but I wasn't going to be known as the cadet who physically couldn't salute.

My path to finding a career I love has been much different than that of my father, but I still see these experiences as a benefit to my professional skill set.

Often, I still feel that the Air Force core values of "integrity first, service before self, and excellence in all we do" continue to motivate me to this day.

This book is a testament to how the military has shaped the lives and careers of many. Each one of these veterans' stories demonstrate how the values and skills taught by military service has been a boon to their careers. Regardless of their branch of service, these men and women have gone on to contribute great things to the energy and utilities industry. By sharing their stories and their advice for companies in the industry, we may come to better understand this extraordinary group of people. This way, we may help to better support their paths to success in the future.

INTRODUCTION

The First Vets in Energy

Westinghouse and Latimer

On October 6, 1846, one of the electric utility industry's greatest founders, George Westinghouse, was born in Central Bridge, New York, the eighth of ten children. That was just twenty-four miles from Schenectady, New York, which ultimately and ironically became the headquarters of Westinghouse's chief rival, the Edison General Electric Company.

Growing up, Westinghouse was hardly easy on his parents. Looking back on this time, he later said, "I have always known what I wanted, and how to get it. As a child, I got it by tantrums; in mature years, by hard work." And as recounted in the 2017 movie *The Current War*, when his father's punishing switch broke during a whipping, Westinghouse pointed out a leather one, saying, "That's a better one, father."

As a teenager, Westinghouse worked in his father's small machine shop in Schenectady, which manufactured agricultural and industrial machinery for fifty cents an hour. But the nation was soon in turmoil and the southern states seceded. Westinghouse ran off to enlist at the age of fifteen, when the war began in 1861. However, his father grabbed the young man right before the train pulled away.

Two years later, in April of 1863, now with his father's approval, Westinghouse enlisted in the Union Army, as a private, serving with Company M the 16th New York Cavalry in the Civil War. He was ultimately promoted to the rank of corporal. The regiment was repeatedly in action in northern Virginia, fighting several fierce engagements against the Confederate irregular cavalry of John Mosby, known as the Gray Ghost. It was not until November of 1864 that Mosby and the commander of Union forces in the Shenandoah Valley, Philip Sheridan, agreed not to execute prisoners.

Westinghouse transferred to the Navy in December of 1864 following the death of a brother killed leading a cavalry charge (after his capture by the

Confederates, confinement at the notorious Libby Prison, and release in a prisoner exchange). Another brother was already in the Navy as an engineering officer. Westinghouse also received a commission as an engineering officer, after passing a special mechanical exam.

He was assigned to a new thirteen-hundred-and-seventy-ton iron side-wheel steam gunboat that entered service in January of 1865, the Mohongo-class U.S.S. Muscoota, as its acting third assistant engineer. In early May of 1865, soon after Lee's surrender at Appomattox Court House and Lincoln's assassination, the Muscoota was dispatched to Key West. The Navy wanted to block the escape of Jefferson Davis, who had been the Confederacy's president.

About this period in his life, Westinghouse wrote: "My earliest, greatest capital was the experience and skill acquired from the opportunity given me when I was young to work with all kinds of machinery, coupled later with lessons in the discipline to which a soldier is required to submit and the acquirement of a spirit of readiness to carry out the instructions of superiors."

Two months after Lee's surrender, on the eleventh of June, while Westinghouse was still eighteen years old, the Muscoota engineering officer received a letter from his father that the Smithsonian Institution has retained in its archives. Westinghouse had received the federal government's approval for his first patent, for a rotary steam engine. His father reported that when the outstanding balance of twenty dollars was paid to the government, the patent would then be issued, which then occurred on the thirty-first of October.

After leaving the Navy in August of 1865, Westinghouse enrolled the next month in Union College, which was and is still located in Schenectady. But he skipped classes to see the most up-to-date machine shops, and to tinker himself, and dropped out before long, staying just three months at the college.

Four years later, Westinghouse became rich and famous for inventing air brakes for railroads. Shaping the energy industry came next.

In the mid-1880s, being impressed by the large production of natural gas from a well on his property, he purchased a gas company. Westinghouse ultimately supplied gas to thousands of homes in Pittsburgh with an extensive pipeline network.

Westinghouse also became interested in electricity. He saw disadvantages to Thomas Edison's direct current-based systems, which prevented a grid of centralized power stations.

Now based in Pittsburgh, Westinghouse acquired exclusive rights to Nikola Tesla's patent for the polyphase system. And lured the volatile inventor to western Pennsylvania to continue his work on alternating current motors.

Westinghouse won the prize contract to light Chicago's Columbian Exposition in 1893. He manufactured over two hundred thousand lamps for lighting and replacements. The Westinghouse exhibit also included a complete working model of a polyphase system, including step-up and step-down transformers, a transmission line, and switch board.

At about the same time, Westinghouse was negotiating to supply alternating current generators, using hydropower at Niagara Falls, to electrify Buffalo, New York. Westinghouse became the successful bidder over six other companies. The historic system went commercial in the fall of 1895.

While Westinghouse was serving on the Mohongo-class U.S.S. Muscoota, as its acting third assistant engineer in the last months of the Civil War and first months of its aftermath, as an eighteen-year-old, Lewis Latimer was serving on the Sassacus-class U.S.S. Massasoit, as a landsman, as a sixteen-year-old. A landsman, commonly called a boy, was the Navy's lowest rank, below that of a seaman. Latimer's Massasoit was a nine-hundred-seventy-four-ton iron side-wheel steam gunboat, smaller than Westinghouse's Muscoota, and it entered service a few months before the Muscoota.

Like Westinghouse a founder of the electric utility industry, Latimer was born on September 4, 1848, in Chelsea, Massachusetts, the last of four children. Like Westinghouse, Latimer was a technical genius throughout his life and became a serial inventor. Unlike Westinghouse, who was of German descent, Latimer was of African descent and the son of escaped slaves.

Westinghouse and Latimer likely knew each other in the late eighteen eighties and early nineties, during which the world's electrification was dominated by the companies of Westinghouse and Thomas Edison. Latimer was Edison's chief draftsman, expert witness in the numerous patent disputes, and lead researcher of scientific developments internationally.

But the two Navy gunboat veterans were certainly acquainted once the Board of Patent Control was established by Westinghouse and Edison in 1896, a rare armistice between the two men, to corner the market on electrical devices. Latimer was made a member of the Board's leadership team.

Latimer is not nearly as well-known as Westinghouse and Edison, who along with Nikola Tesla, are famous for jointly founding the electric utility industry. Nonetheless, this self-taught intellectual giant, who overcame obstacle after obstacle as an African American in the Gilded Age, played a major role in the inventions of the telephone and light bulb.

Latimer considered his military service a foundation for his success. He was an active member in the Grand Army of the Republic from the formation of this veterans' organization. And he was a secretary and adjutant for the group.

Pictured: Jeff Ihnen (top left), Stephanie Roper (top center), Rob Douglass (top right), Kersha Brown (center left), DeAnne Ostrowski (center right), and Brandon Pixley (bottom, right)

Pictured: Brook Bedell (top left), Sophia Eccleston (top center), Jeff Benson (top right), Iliana Rentz (center, second from the left), and Sophia Eccleston (bottom)

Pictured: Kersha Brown (top left), Ron Wild (top right), Sean Grier (center, far right), Iliana Rentz (bottom)

CHAPTER ONE

Joining the Armed Forces

Answering the Call

From the very beginning, when colonial minutemen independently self-taught weapons and strategy in the Revolutionary War, our military has been an integral part of our national identity. Men of all ages answered the call to defend the independence, safety, and welfare of our citizens. But that was 1776. These days, both men and women are joining our armed forces. And the reasons they join are much more complex than the British are coming.

While many were drafted into service during the World Wars, in the decades after, every individual comes to service with a unique origin story. But while every story is indeed unique, many of the veterans in this chapter discuss similar beginnings. Many cite a need for direction, for structure, or even to make a living as being a key reason in their choice to join the military.

As far as recruitment, some truly did stroll into the recruiter's office and ask what opportunities were available. Others came into the office and told them what they were looking to do—and sometimes got swiftly told to dream smaller. Everyone can't be a helicopter pilot straight out of basic after all.

Whether they knew where they wanted to go and how they wanted to do it, or simply asked the recruiter what was on offer, these stories all make one fact very clear: the military has jump-started some incredible careers.

But Wait, There's More...

Brook Bedell graduated high school in 1991 and matriculated to East Tennessee State University, where he majored in mass communications and theater. After living life a little too much to the fullest, he flunked out of college, withdrawing from the university to retain his 1.6 grade point average.

He tried to make it on his own for a year, living with a roommate and selling health club memberships. But he struggled to make ends meet, and when his car broke down, he had no money to repair it. Now, having lost his job and his place to stay, he found himself in 1993 taking shots of Night Train Express with his friends in the small hours of the morning. He looked up with bleary eyes at the TV and saw a U.S. Army recruiting advertisement with the slogan "Be All You Can Be." So, he decided to join up.

After scoring well on his Armed Services Vocational Aptitude Battery, his recruiter asked him what he was interested in doing in the Army. Bedell replied that he wanted to fly helicopters. His recruiter stopped him there, explaining that only officers got to fly helicopters. However, he could work as a door gunner or a mechanic on a helicopter. Bedell was enthusiastic until he heard that it was a six-year commitment. He'd had enough trouble deciding what college to go to for four years. How could he commit to something as unfamiliar as the military for six?

His recruiter then gave him the option to do land survey. He could walk around the woods, hit the plumb bob here, dig there. That sounded nice. But that wasn't all Bedell had signed up for. His ultimate intention was to return to college using the GI Bill. So, what was his bare minimum option to qualify for education benefits?

The only options available were combat arms or infantry. With no knowledge of combat arms and a father who served as a Ranger in Vietnam, he opted for the latter. The commitment was just two years and eight months, but it would secure him twenty thousand dollars for college.

His recruiter then told him, with all the vigor of an As Seen on TV commercial spokesman, that for just four more months, he could get twenty-five thousand dollars for college. Bedell was so poor at the time, he was ready to sign up. So, following in his father's footsteps and stoking his mother's worries, he set off for two years at Fort Hood and later, a year in Korea.

What Are You Wearing?

Jeff Benson grew up the youngest of five kids. Three of his older brothers served during the Vietnam War, and as Benson went through high school, he knew it was going to be college or the service for him. He contacted all the local recruiters for information. But once he graduated, he was offered the chance to play sports at the collegiate level. So, he decided to give college a shot.

During his first year in college, he passed his classes and went through the motions. But he hated it. It was just like high school. There were general courses in math and English and more standard work he was tired of. It was then that Benson started taking a more serious look at the military route. His brothers were in the U.S. Army and the U.S. Air Force. So, how did he end up enlisting in the U.S. Marine Corps? It started out as a question of aesthetics.

He was looking at the uniforms. The Air Force uniform just reminded him of a suit. The Army uniform reminded him of a boy scout or a cub scout uniform. And the Navy…well, he wasn't going to wear bell-bottoms. When he came to the Marine Corps dress blues, he thought the uniform was rather sharp. And plus, he wanted a challenge, so he was ready to join the few, the proud.

In 1986, Benson joined the Marines as a rifleman. After bootcamp, he went to infantry training school at Camp Pendleton and was then assigned to the Marine Security Forces over in Guam. He spent two years there on guard duty for special weapons.

He later received orders to go back to Camp Pendleton with the First Marine Division. He was attached to a company there, where he continued to serve until 1992.

Joining The Team

DeAnne Ostrowski grew up as the child of a U.S. Navy veteran. Her father spent her whole life promoting the military as a great place to start out. Then, as a freshman in high school, she had the privilege of playing on the varsity softball team and befriended a senior on the team who was considering colleges like the Naval Academy, West Point, Rensselaer Polytechnic Institute, and Rochester Institute of Technology.

One day, while she was waiting for practice to start, the senior gave her a catalog for the Naval Academy. She explained that with Ostrowski's background, it might be a great fit. But since Ostrowski was a freshman, she made her promise not to look at it for another two years. This was a promise she wouldn't be able to keep.

She went home that night after practice and started thumbing through the book, reading about all the opportunities she might have. After hearing her dad talk about how great it was to be in the military, she became excited about what could be. But she never thought she would actually get in. When she got her phone call, the Naval Academy was recruiting her for basketball. When she later got her letter, there was no turning back.

She attended the Naval Academy for four years. It was a challenging environment for anybody, but as a woman, Ostrowski stuck out like a sore thumb. Everybody was watching, wanting to form their opinions and see what she did. She always had to be on her game.

After college, she served as a surface warfare officer on two amphibious ships out of Norfolk, Virginia, the Wasp and the Ashland.

The Lifelong Volunteer

When Iliana Rentz was twelve years old, she knew she wanted to be a soldier. She didn't know how, in what capacity, where, or when it would happen, but she knew that she wanted to serve the country and protect our freedoms. Her family had fled Cuba's oppressive government and moved to Spain where she was born, later immigrating to America when she was a child.

Due to this mixing among cultures, her accent is difficult to place. While she claims a Miami accent, if she talks to a Cuban, they tell her she sounds South American. Whereas, if she talks to a South American, they tell her she sounds like a Spaniard. Her Spanish skills were especially formal, as she had grown up reading the Reader's Digest to her grandfather in Spanish. Later, in her military career, she used her Spanish skills as a linguist as well.

In high school, Rentz joined the Junior Reserve Officer Training Corps (ROTC) program and loved it. She joined the drill team, spinning rifles, and also the Ranger team, camping in the woods and rappelling. A fun Friday night for her was going to the Miami Beach Lighthouse after dark, climbing to the top of it, rappelling down into the ocean, and then swimming back.

When she graduated high school, she did ROTC at the University of Miami. During her second year of school, Hurricane Andrew paid Miami a visit. Rentz volunteered immediately, signing up with the Red Cross to do whatever she could to help. They started with search and rescue and also provided aid to tent cities.

During the aftermath of Hurricane Andrew, since schools were going to be closed the next semester, she decided to visit the U.S. Army recruiter and enlist. She took her Armed Services Vocational Aptitude Battery, then came home to tell her friends and family she was leaving that Friday. Everyone laughed at her. But when Friday morning came around, she was starting her journey in the military. Four months later, she was headed to Korea.

On the Drive Home

In 1996, Chad Simon graduated from high school in Atchison, Kansas, a small town on the Missouri River, North of Kansas City. And the last thing he wanted to do in his life at that point was join the military. But his father had spent two years in Vietnam with the U.S. Marine Corps, and he was encouraging Simon to go to Kansas University, just fifty miles away. Why? They had a Reserve Officer Training Corps program there.

Regardless, Simon still had zero interest in the military at the time. His idea was the only way he would join up was the draft. He ended up studying for two and a half years at Fort Hays State University in Hays, Kansas.

He wanted to be a sportswriter, a reporter or a journalist. He even worked in the university relations office and wrote for the school newspaper while he was studying. Unfortunately, he wasn't the best student. He did well in the classes he enjoyed, but for those he didn't, he rarely showed up for class. When he continued not going to class, he started to feel guilty. It was disrespectful to the professors and not conducive to academic success in any way. Eventually, he stopped going to his classes altogether.

Now, he had a four-hour drive home to his parent's house in Atchison. However, his parents had made it clear that moving back home was not going to be an option. During those four hours, he had to think about what his next move would be.

He didn't want to start on a dead-end job because it would be difficult to get back into school at a later point. That's when he took another look at the military. He thought about the military, how his dad had been a Marine, and he decided. Over Thanksgiving he called the Marine Corps recruiter and finished up whatever classes he could salvage from Fort Hays State that semester. In February of 1999, he was off to boot camp.

Detour

Ron Wild moved around a lot growing up due to his father's work. However, he considers Hanna, Wyoming to be where he truly grew up, having moved there around the sixth grade. 1983 saw another era of the Wyoming energy boom-bust cycle. His father came home one day and told the family to pack up, they were leaving. The local coal mine had shut down. Wild only had a few months until his high school graduation at the time, but his father loaded them up and they were on their way to Farmington, New Mexico.

Driving down the road in Farmington, Wild noticed a military recruiting station. His father was in the U.S. Navy and Wild saw no future working in the oil fields or the mines, so he asked his father to pull in. Wild thought maybe he'd join the military, but he knew hardly anything about it at the time.

When he walked in, all the recruiters were out of the office except for the U.S. Air Force. The recruiter showed Wild a recruiting video and he was on board. In October 1983, at seventeen, he took his Armed Services Vocational

Aptitude Battery and scored well enough to follow the path of security police. And there he was, starting a career based on a short stop on a random excursion to town.

Rowing His Boat

Rob Douglass entered the U.S. Navy as a legacy. All three of his uncles and his father were in the Navy. His father, a Naval Academy graduate, was actually a classmate of Jimmy Carter's. In the Navy, his father worked on surface ships and later transitioned into the submarine force via diesel boats. In fact, he was part of Admiral Rickover's original program and worked for the Admiral for a short period of time as one of the first commanding officers of a nuclear submarine back in the 1960s.

Douglass grew up listening to a lot of exciting and interesting stories from his father's time in the Navy, but more importantly, he liked the culture. He would see his father get together with his old submarine buddies. They would sit around and drink martinis, smoke their cigars and pipes, and as his mother used to call it, "row their boats."

Douglass was inspired by their bond. Not to mention that as a child on family vacations, they also had friends in Charleston, South Carolina on the Naval base. Whenever they were visiting, his father was always able to get a tour of a submarine. The proud son was just fascinated.

The academy bug later bit Douglass as well. He eventually graduated from the Naval Academy in 1987 and was selected to become a Naval officer in nuclear power.

Jamaica to Germany

Around 1995, while living in Boston, Sophia Eccleston saw a commercial advertisement for the U.S. Army. Originally from Jamaica, she felt that military service would be a great way to give back to the country that took her in.

She walked into the recruiting office, ready to sign up. Strangely enough, the recruiter told her to go home and think about it, but Eccleston was back the next day. She enlisted at twenty-three years old.

Growing up in Jamaica, she had always been athletic, even doing track and field. But when she went to basic training, she had to walk a little bit during their very first two-mile run. When they got back to the barracks, the first sergeant had every one who stopped to walk doing sprints. That was the last time Eccleston fell out of a run.

Because she was not an American citizen and lacked a college degree, there were certain jobs she wasn't entitled to do. After her aptitude test, she explained to her recruiter that she wanted to commit to service for a maximum of three years.

Her intention was not to pursue the military as a career. She eventually wanted to go back and explore her prospects in the civilian world. The shortest timeframe, two years, gave her the option of becoming a laundry specialist. She quickly denied that offer. Of the few options he gave her next, she decided upon working as a logistics specialist.

She completed her basic training at Fort Jackson, South Carolina and her advanced training at Fort Lee, Virginia over the course of six months. She later secured a station overseas in Germany.

As a country girl from Jamaica, coming to the huge United States and then being sent all the way to Germany was an incredible experience. But it wasn't by random chance. Eccleston had always wanted to go to Germany. When she signed up, she was given a stateside option and an overseas option. In her first, second, and third options, she selected Germany. And she loved it.

She was originally stationed in Heidelberg, Germany during the conflict in Bosnia. She was responsible for ensuring her company was constantly supplied and that all weapons were accounted for. She also oversaw supply chain schedules, coordinating efforts to ensure all supplies and equipment were sent to and received by deployed units. Her company and battalion even deployed to Bosnia at that time, although Eccleston did not go herself. Her role was supporting them through logistics, staying back to manage the supply room while her supply sergeant was deployed.

Eccleston spent two years in Germany, even having her first child while she was serving there. But she knew that she needed to come back to the United States, rather than stay overseas, so she could transition back into society a bit better. So, she extended her time there an additional six months, and was then transferred back to the United States.

Changing Paths

Stephanie Roper comes from a deeply rooted military family, having uncles and grandfathers who served in either the U.S. Navy or the U.S. Air Force. Growing up, she never really saw herself going that route. As a high school senior in Austin, Texas, she applied to college at the University of Texas and Texas A&M. Her parents told her that if she went to the University of Texas she would have to live at home. Naturally, as a seventeen-year-old pursuing her own freedom, she decided to go to Texas A&M to study business administration. She wasn't sure exactly what she wanted to do with that, but she had chosen a path.

One day, during her senior year of high school in 1991, Roper was walking between classes and a U.S. Army recruiter stopped her to ask if she had ever considered enlisting. She wasn't interested, but he asked if she would stop by the Army's recruiting presentation later that day. She decided to go and see what he had to say, out of respect. She sat down and watched the recruiting video and found herself thinking it was the coolest thing she'd ever seen. And that was it.

Roper took her Armed Services Vocational Aptitude Battery and was offered a litany of positions. One that shocked her was a role as a heavy wheel vehicle mechanic, which was surprisingly where she drew her highest score. She had a few more options to explore, but more importantly, she needed her parents' permission to enlist at seventeen.

That evening, she went home, and her mother was so distraught to hear that she was ready to enlist in the Army and not the Air Force. Despite her mother's hesitancy, Roper signed the papers. Within a week, she had enlisted in the Delayed Entry Program as part of the U.S. Army Reserve. She started drilling in the Army Reserve one weekend each month until she graduated from high school, when she finally went away to basic training and Advanced Individual Training in Columbia, South Carolina. She graduated as part of the last cohort prior to the gender integration of the Army basic training program.

A Break from School

As Kersha Brown was taking AP classes and finishing high school, she realized that she didn't want to go straight to college. She wanted a break, but she knew she couldn't just sit at home. Her mother was not going to have that at all. The answer came to her high school in the form of Army recruiters. She signed up for the aptitude test and even signed some initial paperwork, all without her mother's knowledge. When it eventually came out that she was joining the Army, her mother was shocked, but she eventually came around to the idea.

Brown officially enlisted in 1999. She recalls basic training as a mental exercise. If you're mentally strong, they train you physically. But the whole class of physical training is being able to get through it. Her chosen Military Occupational Specialty was seventy-seven (later changed to ninety-two) Foxtrot, a job as a petroleum fuel specialist.

During her time in the military, she was activated once after the 9/11 terrorist attacks. When she first received orders for deployment, they sent her to Watertown, New York to train with the mountain division. However, after months of training, a week before it was time to take off, their mission was canceled. In a way, she was grateful that she didn't have to experience a deployment oversees. Many of her comrades and battle buddies who did end up going over were different in a lot of ways upon their return.

Pictured: Brook Bedell (top left), Rick Rother (top center), Stephanie Roper (top right), Joe Tolbert (center left), Ming-wa Hui (center right, far right), Scott Bolton (bottom, middle)

Pictured: Monique Carter (top left), Rob Douglass (top center), Scott Bolton (top right), Kevin Hernandez (center left), Jeff Benson (center right, far right), Mike Rich (bottom left, holding flag on right), Brad Vander Plas (bottom right)

CHAPTER TWO

In the Military

Work-Life Balance

When we think of the military, many of us think of gun-toting, camo-clad GI Joe with characteristic haircuts. But there is a vast array of roles for men and women to take up in the service. There are jobs that utilize skills not only in strength, but in strategy, be it hazardous war zones or human relations. While some service members spend their time carrying out missions with special forces, still others are working in communications or media.

Not only was their role in the military a job, but it was also a lifestyle. It's often complicated navigating a life off base, or otherwise complicated having work and personal lives so closely mingled on base. But it isn't all downsides.

For instance, military personnel receive extensive leadership training in the service, whether directly or indirectly. Exposure to a variety of leaders and leadership styles informs the professional skills they carry with them as they separate from their branch of service.

In this chapter, we'll recount the stories of what some of the utilities industry's veterans were doing during their time in the armed forces. Whether they were stateside or globe-trotting, each of their jobs taught them unique lessons and skills that they bring to the energy and utilities industry today.

Service in Spades

Frank Bailey joined the U.S. Army in the fall of 2008, finishing up basic training right around Christmastime. He was trained as a truck mechanic, Military Occupational Specialty code 63-Bravo. However, in 2009, he was attached to the 5/158th battalion in Germany, with an aviation unit. He ended up as a door gunner on a CH-47 Chinook. It was a whole different atmosphere from the ground to the aviation sites.

But how did a truck mechanic end up as a door gunner? Bailey and a few other mechanics were attached to the Charlie Company's medevac operations, and someone was asking for volunteers for door gunners. Bailey was selected and with a bit of training, he was in the left door.

When they weren't in the air, it was his responsibility to clean and load all the machine guns, keep the aircraft clean, and keep emergency provisions on board. He and other door gunners, also mechanics, would take care of all of the maintenance on board as well. They would do everything from delivering mail to emergency support and resupply.

In June of 2009, Bailey and his battalion were deployed in Afghanistan, moving from Kandahar to Shindand over the course of a few months. He was then transported to Bravo Company for the next seven months of his tour.

He describes his time in the Middle East as living in cowboy country. In the western part of Afghanistan, on base in Shindand, local nationals were the gatekeepers on the fence around the compound. Bailey and his comrades couldn't even speak their language. They eventually got a translator, but it was weeks after they had arrived. Meanwhile, it was a struggle deciding whether to trust the locals or the Afghan police, who were often corrupt.

But it wasn't always so serious. Bailey admits that he got pretty good at spades, playing cards with his friends during their downtime. Another in his unit actually set up an internet connection using a satellite dish. It was slow, but with no other options available, Bailey and others paid him for internet connection. However, the connection was bad and half the time they couldn't connect, so there was sometimes a line of thirty guys waiting for reconnection help.

The Return to Arms

Let's return to Brook Bedell's service. After he got out of the U.S. Army in 1996, Bedell went to Truett McConnell University, a small private community college, to raise his grade point average just enough to transfer to the University of Georgia the following year.

But restarting school as a junior left him with the all-important decision of declaring a new major. He couldn't think of anything he was good at besides being a soldier. With a new fiancée on his arm, he thought to himself that the military might give him both benefits and an opportunity to fly. So, Bedell returned to service.

After doing well on his flight aptitude skills test, in 2000, he was the only Lieutenant in his class to be commissioned to go to Fort Rucker, Alabama. During his year at Fort Rucker, he learned how to fly the OH-58 Delta, or Kiowa Warrior.

This armed reconnaissance helicopter was fitted with two and three-quarter-inch rockets and fifty-caliber machine guns. Flying with the doors off, with guns rattling on his left and rockets on his right, he says you would have to be dead not to enjoy it. Up in the sky with his eyeballs rattling, he was in love.

Bedell's first assignment was in early 2001 Germany. He had planned to do six or seven years and get out again, but his prior service put him halfway through. It was time for some math.

With three years of prior service and a six-year aviation commitment, the earliest he could get out of the military would be around the nine-year mark. Then in 2004, he saw the writing on the wall for drones. He put in a fixed-wing application and got picked up to fly airplanes for military intelligence, a five-year commitment. More math.

Now, the soonest he could leave the military was at year fourteen. Later in 2008 while fighting in Iraq, Bedell qualified for a tax free thirty-five-thousand-dollar bonus as an aviator. An additional three-year commitment. Now, the soonest he could get out was at seventeen years.

So, what started off as doing tricks and enjoying himself, had turned into another eleven years in the Army. By then, he knew he was a lifer. He took the bonus and turned it into a slightly used Yukon Denali for his wife and a brand new 2008 Harley Road Glide for himself.

There were several situations during his time in Iraq that called for flight. More often than not, as soon as they got off the ground, their chaff would ignite, meaning that they were being tracked or traced by somebody. Bedell, being forward in the cockpit, didn't know if they were shooting at him or not. Not to mention that for the first four months in the country, they were only authorized to land in Balad.

Flying ten thousand feet overhead, he would immediately have to do an Emergency Descent, which configures the aircraft for propellers high rotations per minute, flaps set at approach with gear down, and not to exceed one hundred seventy-nine knots. After a corkscrew spin over the air base, he could finally come out over the runway, where it was protected, and turn on his lights to land. This roller coaster routine was scary the first six or seven times, but soon enough it was standard.

Later in 2013, Bedell was sent to Afghanistan. He experienced a certain peace and serenity there that he never had anywhere else. As the token aviator in the future planning cell for International Security Assistance Forces as part of the North Atlantic Treaty Organization (NATO) in Kabul, he had several trips to the ministry of defense or to the Afghan army, in which they would travel in an undisclosed car. They sometimes even had battle armor on, but there was nowhere to go, and anybody could put a sticky bomb on the side of that car. They even could have thrown a grenade on the car and there was nothing Bedell and his team could have done. The whole time he was there, every trip could have been the end, and he had to make his peace with that.

But while he understood the sense of anxiety or frustration that his next position might cost him his life, when he was packed in a car and going through downtown Kabul, there was that certain serenity to it. He told himself if God wanted him then, he would simply take him.

Afghanistan was Bedell's favorite deployment because, in 2010, he went to Command General Staff College where he got his Master's in International Relations through Webster University. He was able to apply his degree in the future operation cell with NATO, where a group of thirty officers were working together.

They had the Danes, the Swedes, the Brits, the Canucks, the Aussies, the Kiwis, the Spaniards—everybody. They were all one big family, and it was a good time. As the token aviator with the Brits and the Aussies, Bedell would sometimes read operation orders and shout out in the room that someone had misspelled 'neighbor' or 'realization.' The Brits would stand up and insist it was the Queen's English.

More importantly, this post was an opportunity to learn about one another, to truly work on the personal aspect of international relations. Regardless of speaking different languages, they all had the same problems. He recounts sitting with an Italian army colonel. Bedell asked him if something was wrong. The colonel just looked at him, took a drag of his cigarette, and mused that his daughter's boyfriend was no good for her. Bedell reflected then that we really are all the same. We all have the same trials and tribulations. And that was what he truly enjoyed about this post. He still has friends from his remarkable Afghanistan experience to this day.

Far Traveler

As we returned to Bedell, let's return to Jeff Benson's time in the U.S. Marine Corps. While Benson's post was at Camp Pendleton, he had the opportunity to do a great deal of traveling in the Marines. He had his first West Pacific Cruise, or WESTPAC, out of California while deployed on a U.S. Navy ship. He was in Hawaii numerous times, but he also went to Australia, Guam, Hong Kong, Japan, the Philippines, Singapore, and South Korea.

When he was later deployed in Operations Desert Shield and Desert Storm, his unit was the last to stay in the region as a force in readiness. Throughout his time in the Middle East, he trained in and traveled across

Abu Dhabi, Bahrain, Kuwait, Oman, Qatar, Saudi Arabia, and areas off the coast of Somalia.

Benson's two deployments were on a tank landing ship. These vessels were designed to run aground on a beach, with ramps deployable from the front or back end of the ship. The idea was to drive equipment right out of the ship and onto the beach.

During Desert Storm, there was a force of Navy ships keeping Saddam Hussein's troops in Kuwait City. U.S. Forces had enemy forces believing the invasion was going to come from the sea. Benson was part of the forces that performed the feint invasion against Hussein's troops in Kuwait City. However, he and his fellow troops were unaware that they were the feint. He and others were told to expect eighty-percent casualties hitting the beach.

They ended up landing just on the Kuwait-Saudi Arabia border as the ground war started. Benson recounts having artillery shot at him and his fellow troops. Luckily, it fell short of them, but as it did, a scud missile was shot out of the sky above them.

They later breached numerous minefields and then ended up on road patrol. Because there were so many minefields, once a road was established, everyone used it because it was confirmed safe. Benson ended up patrolling for a day so that they could be sure the enemy wasn't coming back and remining it as they left.

His next assignment was responding to reports of sniper fire. Helicopter pilots would report sniper fire from small towns and villages, then Benson and his team would respond to these locations from the ground as part of a mechanized amphibious unit in Amphibious Assault Vehicles. Their goal being to gain a strategic foothold in one corner of the community.

Intelligence Choice

Without a clear pathway to college after high school, Scott Bolton was struggling to decide what he wanted to do. Coming from a family tradition of military service, he chose to join the U.S. Army. Not only was there some familiarity there, as his father had been a soldier as well, but the Army was also the only service at the time that was guaranteeing your Military Occupational Specialty. If you signed up for a specific job, had the aptitude, and passed your schooling, you would have that job.

He enlisted to be a Signals Intelligence Analyst. As a delayed entry, it was a full year before he left for the Army. In 1989, two weeks after high school graduation, he was on his way to basic training at Fort Leonard Wood, Missouri.

After Intelligence school, his first duty assignment was with the National Security Agency (NSA). He went straight to Fort Meade. For an intelligence analyst, it was a dream come true. There were polygraph tests before he obtained his security clearance and continually rigorous security protocols thereafter.

His first job was a Southeast Asian insurgency mission. American forces were watching the last throes of the Cambodian Civil War and the demise of the Khmer Rouge. However, the Iraqi invasion of Kuwait threw everything into turmoil. Like many other analysts, he immediately found himself working on that mission during the Persian Gulf War, and watched the conflict play out in real time. He saw everything from targeting enemy sites to monitoring intelligence and communications.

The amount of responsibility given to him as a nineteen-year-old was transformational. For Bolton, and likely many others, if was nearly impossible to look past the gravity of the work he was doing.

Meanwhile, there was a constant and intense paranoia about being compromised by foreign powers. It was a very heavy atmosphere, where national security was constantly at stake. Even his ability to talk about his day with his roommate or friends in his barracks was incredibly limited.

He spent two years at the NSA and then the Army sent him to Camp Humphreys in Korea. Because of his previous work, he received a great deal of respect at the field station in Korea and his understanding of how the intelligence gathering pieces fit together was more robust. His experience had been accelerated remarkably during his time at Fort Meade.

Around the time of his being stationed in Korea, he had recently started dating the woman who would later become his wife and who was also in the military. Bolton describes their separation as brutal. If had been single at the time, he might have been more interested in re-enlisting. However, as it was, the minute he got to Korea, his mind was fixated on how to get back home.

One for the Photo Books

Kelcey Brown's family background gave her a strong inclination towards military service. With several family members having served in the U.S. Navy and the U.S. Army, she realized that military service would be a great way to pay for college. However, when she decided to join the Navy, it was initially a shock to her family. After being told by her recruiter that she'd have to do more school first to become a pilot and much deliberation on her options, she enlisted as a photographer.

She committed to five years and shipped off to boot camp in Orlando, Florida. In fact, she was part of the last class to graduate there, and the facility has since been closed. She then went to Pensacola, Florida for her advanced training.

She ended up as one of the first women on the USS Nimitz aircraft carrier. There were twenty-five women among a crew of five thousand. There were only two women's bathrooms on the entire ship.

As a photographer on board the ship, she had access to two different photo labs. She and the other photographers maintained all their own equipment and chemistry necessary to fulfill their station. One lab was close to operations, developing film that came off reconnaissance planes. She and others would mount these cameras underneath planes and later develop film and make prints of useful images. The other lab was a more regular photo lab for working with an array of photo opportunities.

She photographed many ceremonies and events, everything from changes of command to re-enlistments. She also covered a few burials at sea. And if there were damaged parts, accidents, injuries, crimes, or investigations on the ship, she would get called for that too. Then, whenever they stopped at port, they would take photos for the cruise book. And she also took headshots for both officers and enlisted personnel on board.

There was also a media component to her role as a shooter for photography. They would often do a photo of the day or send off photos to various publications. They might even have dignitaries on board, and on these occasions, they would follow them and make a photo book.

For her first two and a half years on the ship, Brown would have her camera in-hand as she went around, taking photos everywhere she went. For the next two and a half years after that, she worked on large photography prints, much of her time spent in the dark room.

Brown was often aboard her ship for months at a time, but this gave her some unique travel opportunities. While many times they were refueled at sea by supply ships, she got the chance to visit Dubai, Hong Kong, Japan, Singapore, and Thailand.

Miss Independent

Monique Carter started her work in the U.S. Air Force as a ground radio operator. On her first base, she was stationed in a mobility unit. Nowadays, these units no longer exist, but they were a popular fixture in the Air Force back in the day.

Carter served in a combat communications group. The whole thing was a challenge, especially with her first unit being a mobility unit. It required her and the rest of her unit to go out to the field. However, a lot of times they did not have to sleep in tents in the Air Force. In fact, they would usually stay in some old, unused barracks. Even when they did sleep out in a tent, as airmen, they would be brought hot meals for breakfast and dinner. The facilities group also provided them with shower tents for men and for women. Carter was able to have a nice, hot shower every day. But even with all the luxuries the Air Force afforded her, she was not at all used to using a port-a-potty.

But she was also soaking in the culture of the military. Although raised by a stern single mother, the forms of authority and tasks in the Air Force were unfamiliar to her. She wasn't opposed to authority but some of the things that the military requested of her didn't always make sense. For her to challenge any authority was its own challenge. To this day, she considers herself a very vocal person, but also believes she has matured in how she vocalizes. Back then in the Air Force, at nineteen, things were very different.

During Carter's four years, nineteen days, and nine-hour career in the Air Force, she was stationed at three bases. She started off at Patrick Air Force Base in Florida, by Cape Canaveral. She volunteered for a worldwide remote tour, which meant that she received orders quickly, but the tour was only for one year.

So, she went to Greece, where there were less than a hundred people at her site. However, her home base was in Athens, nearly three and a half hours away. Her time in Greece was considered a remote assignment. When her year in Greece was up, she was sent to Barksdale Air Force Base in Shreveport, Louisiana.

Many say that their time in the military made them more timely, more mature, or that it helped them to grow up. However, Carter believes that it was her mother who instilled the majority of those values in her prior to her service. What the military taught her was how to be independent. She joined the military at nineteen years old, gaining her independence and buying her own brand new red 1987 Nissan Sentra.

When Carter was in the military, she never really considered doing a whole twenty years. A lot of her friends had already decided that was their path, but she was unsure. She finally decided she would do her four years and that would be it. But when she separated from the Air Force, she had zero idea of what she was going to do.

Following the Script

So, whatever happened to Rob Douglass after he graduated from the Naval Academy? Well, he knew he wanted to go into nuclear power. So, he set up his Naval service selection accordingly and got into engineering. He focused on nuclear for as much of his studies at the Academy as he could.

Upon the start of the selection process, Admiral Rickover had since been succeeded by Admiral McKee. McKee didn't grill Douglass extensively as he had feared, but he did note that Douglass had managed to pull off an A in his thermodynamics course. Douglass attributed that feat to having the right teacher, as another in the same course was notorious for failing midshipmen. Overall, the discussion was short and to the point, tamed down from the rough stories he had heard of Admiral Rickover's selections.

After being selected to go to the University of Michigan right away following graduation, Douglass went into the nuclear engineering program. Later, it was off to six months at the Navy Nuclear Power School in Orlando, Florida. Later still, he spent another six months at the prototype S1C reactor in Windsor, Connecticut. After submarine school, he was off to his first ship, the USS James K. Polk, a ballistic missile submarine out of Charleston, South Carolina.

The Polk was home for three years. They made strategic deterrent patrols out of Holy Loch, Scotland. From there, he started sea-shore rotations with his assignments. It was typically three years on the ship, then two years on shore, and repeat. And if he got selected to the next level up, the rotation would change.

On his first ship, it was a very scripted life with the watch rotation. The predictability of the ballistic missile submarines was pizza night every Saturday. They all slept in on Sunday and would try to go to church too. Although there were also administrative tasks to complete on Sundays.

Overall, it was a comfortable rhythm. But they were always counting down the seventy-five or eighty days until the patrol would be over. There was even a time where they were continuously submerged for nearly eighty days.

But his time underway was always interesting. He was always learning, and there was always so much to learn, like the reactor plant and watch standing. After getting reactor operator qualifications in the engine room, it was on to the "front" (or forward part) of the boat to work on tactical training: driving the ship, shooting torpedoes, fighting the ship.

Your qualifications on the ship had a very scripted progression. You were first put in charge of a nuclear division of Sailors, including either electrical division, mechanical division, reactor controls division, or chemical radiological assistants. All those things would contribute later in his life to going into the civilian nuclear power business.

Back in port in Charleston, the Polk was eventually converted into a dry dock shelter, where Douglass and the rest of his crew performed SEAL delivery, including having a mini submarine barn on top of what used to be missile tubes. They later ended up hauling Navy SEALs around to be able to covertly insert and extract them.

Douglass also got to see some shipyard time at Portsmouth Naval Shipyard. There, he got familiar with the maintenance side of the reactor steam generator inspections, and much higher anti-contamination, radiological controls that you typically don't see in an operational submarine. All this on his very first three-year tour.

His next ship was the USS Pittsburgh, and his follow-on ship was the USS Louisiana. It was a formal selection process and still quite structured. But Douglass had a lot of great mentors and really enjoyed what he was doing. However, he was spending a lot of time away from home, which was tough on his family.

Command was the pinnacle of his career, where he and his ship, the USS Albuquerque, had the opportunity to make two forward deployments in support of national tasking in the Southern Command and Central Command (Persian Gulf) Areas of Responsibility. The USS Albuquerque steamed nearly eighty thousand miles during his two and a half years in command.

When he finally reached his twenty-year mark, he hadn't had a chance to really get to know his two sons, who were still young elementary schoolers. It was time to shift gears. He was selected for the next round of promotions for Navy captain, but he needed a good quantity of quality time with his family. He then decided to transition into commercial nuclear power and retired from the Navy in 2007. But as he had throughout his Navy career, he had a plan.

Throughout his time in the Navy, there were career review boards for all sailors and junior officers while underway. Sailors would come in to talk to the chief, the supervisor, the chain of command, and discuss their skills and technical qualifications and how they might translate into next steps like furthering education and civilian careers.

FirstEnergy became Douglass' utility of choice as it was in Ohio. Both he and his wife grew up in the state, and they wanted their sons to enjoy a similar experience growing up in the Midwest. He had done his homework, too. After going through the courses on various job-hunting skills like resume writing and interview techniques, he armed himself with knowledge on what opportunities would be available to him in the civilian world and started networking.

He searched the Service Academy equivalent of LinkedIn at the time for Naval Academy and other service academy graduate contacts in nuclear utility, and almost everyone he sent an email to got back with him within a week and offered their help and assistance. The director of performance improvement at FirstEnergy's Perry Nuclear Power Plant was among them. After seeing Douglass' email, cover letter, and resume, he called. They were looking for someone to start immediately.

Douglass started at FirstEnergy's Corporate Headquarters in Akron, Ohio, in Fleet Work Management. He also worked at the Perry Nuclear Power Plant during several outages as a Project Manager including Chemical Decontamination of the Reactor during one outage and as the Integrated Containment Management Manager for another. He then transitioned into the Senior Reactor Operator pipeline, received his SRO certification, and transitioned into safety and human performance at the corporate level including taking the nuclear High Reliability Organizing culture into the Fossil Fleet. He was Acting Director of safety and human performance for nuclear generating fleet before leaving FirstEnergy at the end of 2016.

The Second Career

Ming-wa Hui received his engineering degree from the University of Colorado, Boulder in 1999 and started a career with Xcel Energy shortly after. He joined Xcel Energy not actually having a power systems background. So, he went back to graduate school at the University of Colorado, Denver while he was working.

In the middle of graduate school and getting his professional engineering license, the terrorist attack of 9/11 occurred. At the end of 2003, Hui was about to graduate and had just finished exams for his engineering license. It was the holiday season, and while he was watching the news, he saw holiday messages from deployed personnel and military families. They were sending messages to their fathers, mothers, daughters, and sons. Hui was single at the time, sitting in his condo. He thought to himself, he had to go serve.

Hui had literally zero exposure to the military and nobody in his family had ever served before. All he knew was the state of Colorado had a National Guard. He would be able to serve in the Army and work at the same time. He simply walked into an office in Lakewood, Colorado, gave the recruiter his credentials, and asked what he qualified for.

That's where everything fell into place. When he was talking with the recruiter about what he should do, Hui told him he wanted to do anything but engineering. He already had an engineering job. He wanted to do something that would give him a learning experience.

Being fluent in Chinese, Hui thought that they could perhaps use his language skills. The recruiter explained that in Colorado at the time, there were only two units that would use his language. One was Special Operations Korea, and the other was the 19th Special Forces Group.

Hui didn't know at all what either really meant at the time, but he caught the word 'Korea' and thought it would make sense for his language skills. The recruiter had other ideas and steered Hui's interest towards being in the 19th Special Forces Group covering Southeast Asia. Still knowing little about the military, Hui trusted the recruiter's judgment. In hindsight, he might have paid more attention when he was asked whether he would be okay with jumping out of airplanes.

Hui joined the 19th Special Forces Group in 2003, arriving at his unit for the first time in July. He had no idea who to go talk to. Incidentally, he got caught up in selection for the Green Berets by accident until his recruiter found him. He quickly redirected Hui to his actual unit, but the transition into his real work wasn't nearly as fast.

Unfortunately, he was put on hold until the next basic combat course in October. Until he went to basic training, he was going to drill with the unit every month as an officer candidate, Military Occupational Specialty (MOS) code 09-Sierra. His secondary MOS was as a signal intelligence operator because of his language skills.

He ended up working with a small intelligence group finding targets and doing tactical training. His first exposure to the military was outdoor survival and rigorous physical fitness work. He was running around the mountains of Colorado, camping, hiding, and testing his survival skills. Unbeknownst to him, he was undergoing Special Forces training.

When October finally came, he went through basic training and then immediately started Officer Candidate School. There, he quickly learned that as an officer, he would be pushing paper. Hui did not want that. He thought back to his training. All the drills he did, the new skills he had learned. He wasn't about to waste all that pushing paper. So, he resigned his spot in the Officer Candidate School and stayed enlisted. He wanted to be an operator in the field, the boots on the ground.

From 2004 to 2006, Hui was supposed to get his top-secret clearance for his intelligence job as an operator. For some inexplicable reason, his paperwork kept getting lost somewhere in the clearance system for those two years. This left him in the Army for two years with no MOS. Almost half his contract was spent with no Advanced Individual Training completed and no active job post. He couldn't do a job because he wasn't qualified for any. He reflects that they must have liked him enough to keep him while he simply trained and hung about.

Finally, in 2006, they told him to find a new vocation. Hui chose to go to medic school. He reasoned that if he followed that path all the way through, he could get into an official position with the unit. Later that same year, he went down to Fort Sam Houston to train as a combat medic. After he completed combat medic school, he went to Fort Benning for airborne school and completed his airborne qualifications to become a qualified paratrooper. He was then sent to Fort Bragg to initiate training to become the unit's Green Beret. And he was psyched.

But that elation was short-lived. For several months at Fort Bragg, there was a shortage of trainers because Special Operation Operators were needed to cover the war. There weren't enough instructors to constantly train people at the time. A traditional medic path takes about two to three years to qualification, but the shortage of trainers was so severe that Hui could have been stuck there for five years completing his coursework.

He still had his secondary MOS at that point, as a signal intelligence operator. But he now also had a qualified MOS as a medic, so he was able go back to his unit. He decided to return to Colorado as a medic, and sort things out there. He had a potential back-up plan of being a flight medic, as there was a flight medic unit in Colorado as well. He was just itching to serve.

Hui served in Louisiana during the aftermath of Hurricane Katrina. He and others provided security for a month, in New Orleans, but shortly after that, the unit got called up to go to Iraq. He was able to stay on as a medic, not with an official post but still with an official job. He was still allowed to deploy, but there were no medic slots in a Special Forces unit, only medic operators. They gave him the option to stay on the Signal Intelligence team of four as its team medic.

For eight months, Hui and his unit traveled across Southern Iraq from Baghdad to Basra. They supported Scraper A-Teams hunting high-value targets, guiding the Direct Action Team to the correct locations at the correct time. Hui was part of the team supporting all of Southern Iraq in 2007 for a Special Operations Team Alpha team with the 5th Special Forces Group.

He says his first deployment was phenomenal, albeit nerve-racking and somewhat overwhelming. His first mission was a quick reactionary force mission to save the local SWAT team police chief from assassination by local insurgents using a vehicle Improvised Explosive Device. Hui got out of the truck and the ground was full of shells. They were shooting like crazy already by the time he and his team got there. He took a knee and looked out, but the Iraqi police didn't wear uniforms, they were simply standing around with AK-47s. It was nearly impossible to tell who the enemy was in this urban environment. Who was he supposed to shoot? Who was going to shoot him? He adjusted as he went.

He learned over the next eight months that special operations deployments are short relative to one year of deployment. Units become very competitive in each eight-month period, every unit wanting to be the most productive special ops unit in that region. The tempo was very high, and Hui and his unit were leaving the base almost every night to try to hunt down as many people as possible. He learned a lot about being bold, working constant twelve to fourteen-hour shifts. In his twenty-four-hour operation, many tasks were life or death.

There were many lessons to experience in Special Forces, but Hui believed that they were well worth it. He felt he needed to endure the heartaches experienced by many of the young people who join the Army. When he first joined, he looked at the TV and saw a lot of younger people. He was young at the time at twenty-five, but most of them were seventeen or eighteen years old. And when he went through basic training with them, he watched these adolescents completely lose their freedom just to serve their country. As a unit, they simply worked on trying to support each other. But Hui also learned a lot about the passion of our veterans and what they endure, especially the sacrifices they and their families make.

Hui says the value of selfless service taught to him by the military was tremendous. That's what he will always take with him. But being willing to do anything to accomplish the task carries out so much more in the civilian world, he believes. It's about being willing to do things that other people don't like to do but are necessary for an organization. Hui also learned about leadership, how to lead from the front, by example. These are the values he took away from the military and back to the civilian workforce when he got the chance.

The last part of his service after the war, Hui was just thankful to survive a war. He was ready for a career now, ready to build his life. He got married and started a family, and his wife was not going to be home with two kids while he was gone most of the year.

When he got out of the signal intelligence group, he became an Imagery Analyst. It was an office job. No longer did he have to hump miles and miles with heavy gear outdoors. He tried to convince his wife it was an office job, it would slow down, but he reflects that it didn't slow down as much as she would have liked it to. It was at that point Hui finally decided to wrap up his military career.

Looking For Excitement

Ramon Mitchell graduated from Reed College in 2009 with a bachelor's degree in economics. After graduating, he didn't feel like simply getting a desk job. He was young. He wanted to be something, do something exciting, go on a grand adventure. So, he thought, why not join the U.S. Army? At the time, he thought it couldn't get more exciting than that.

As he was going through the process at first, he had wanted to be an officer. When he went to the recruiter, however, they explained that only citizens of the United States could be officers. As a Jamaican immigrant, although he held a green card, Mitchell was ineligible.

He took his aptitude test and earned good scores. He could have been a medic, a truck driver, or work in intelligence. The recruiter was confused when he said he wanted to do infantry. They suggested he become a combat engineer, explaining that it was kind of like infantry, but he would work with explosives. That sounded even cooler.

In 2010, he enlisted as an active-duty combat engineer. He completed his basic training in Missouri and was then stationed at Joint Base Lewis-McChord near Seattle, Washington, where he was assigned to the 22nd Engineer Clearance Company, 14th Combat Engineer Battalion, 555th Engineer Brigade. All of it excited Mitchell, training to neutralize explosives. He knew in the background that they could deploy him, and it would be dangerous, but he was young and feeling invincible.

In June of 2011, Mitchell deployed to Kandahar, Afghanistan for a whole year, just six months after being assigned to his duty station. He worked to ensure the mobility of coalition forces by neutralizing explosive hazards along coalition routes and areas as part of counter-explosive efforts in the region, a job better known as route clearance. He would drive up and down the coalition route, searching for hidden explosives buried under the ground.

Towards the end of his time there, the excited mentality had worn off and the feeling of invincibility was gone. He now had a more realistic, even fatalistic mentality. This was a real combat situation, and his team was relying on him to keep everyone safe.

Even with their best efforts, his company had at least one incident with an Improvised Explosive Device daily. Although, the vehicles they used were designed to take an explosion from underneath. Each vehicle is structured with a V-shaped bottom and designed to break apart and diffuse the impact of the explosion.

During his year in Afghanistan, Mitchell's company went through over seventy vehicles. But there were many more explosives found. Several soldiers were wounded in action, but the most common injury was mild trauma to the brain, basically a concussion. Mitchell was lucky never to be seriously injured by any of these incidents.

Change of Heart

When Mike Rich was in high school, he took the Armed Services Vocational Aptitude Battery (ASVAB) for extra credit. He had no desire to join the military at the time. But a few years after graduation, the 9/11 terrorist attack occurred. The event turned his thinking around, and he recalled that he had done fairly well on the ASVAB in high school. He decided that the military would be a great way to both serve his country and pay for college, so he went straight to the recruiting office and signed up for the U.S. Army in 2003.

At Fort Knox, they shaved his head, sent him through eight weeks of basic training, and then straight on to Fort Lee Virginia for tech school. He chose to work in logistics, because those roles had the shortest tech school training and the highest signing bonus. After six weeks, he was a newly minted Shower and Laundry Technician, on his way to focusing on college again. Little did he know, he would be on orders for deployment just six months later.

At joint base San Antonio, he prepared for his mobilization to Iraq. In November of 2004, he started a year-long deployment where he didn't touch any showers or laundry besides his own. The whole time he was thrown into convoy security, supporting combat logistics patrols, and escorting supply convoys from the Kuwait and Jordanian borders into Iraq.

At the time, Iraq was establishing its first democratic vote. Rich's first four months there, he escorted shipments of jersey barriers being brought into Fallujah to protect polling places from attacks. He was enjoying the experience until the first Improvised Explosive Device (IED) went off in April of 2005. It changed his whole perspective on deployment. At first, it had been a lot of fun having all these new and exciting experiences, but after the explosion, things became much more serious. The insurgency was growing, trying to attack American soldiers in any way possible.

Rich even lost a few friends along the way. They lost three soldiers, two female and one male. The one toughest for him was the loss of their medic. She was deployed as medical support on some of their convoys and she was only in the country for two weeks. She had just sent her first letter home to her family when her vehicle was struck by an IED while in route to support a convoy of Marines who were ambushed nearby.

Rich continues to serve as a reservist to this day. He splits time between the Army and a full-time career at American Water.

Combat Photographer

When Chad Simon enlisted in the U.S. Marine Corps in February of 1999, he had hoped to use his skills as a journalist. But what he did not know at the time, and later found out, was even if you join the Marines and get through boot camp, that doesn't mean you'll get the job you wanted. Your job must be available to start work. And there aren't very many journalism jobs in the Marines. At the time he was looking for one, they were full. So, he was offered a job as a combat photographer. He had taken a class in high school and thought it was fun and interesting, so he agreed.

He later found that photography is his absolute passion and he loved being outdoors in a Marine Corps environment. His school was in Fort Meade, Maryland, and it included personnel from all branches of the military. It was eight hours a day of photography. They also had students working in journalism, video broadcasting, graphic design, and reproduction (generally reprinting military material). He studied there for around three months until he got his first duty station in Yuma, Arizona.

During his time in the Marines, he was kept to the same rigorous standards even though he was a photographer. He and his peers were trained and qualified as riflemen and took the same physical fitness tests and training as every other Marine. They even had to suffer through the gas chamber every year.

Back when Simon originally joined the Marine Corps, there were only three combat cameras in the Marines: First Marine Division, Second Marine Division, and Okinawa, Japan. At some point, the Marine Corps decided to name all the photo and video and graphic sections. These days, it might be called the training and audio-visual center, Simon reflects. But when he was in Yuma, he would perform photo coverage for the Special Reactions Team, the military equivalent of a SWAT team, and military police.

There were a variety of occasions that required Simon's skills as a photographer. Any kind of investigation, whether it was an aircraft mishap or the death of a fellow Marine, he would be there recording the events with his camera. At that point, they were still using film cameras and the people who knew how to use them were few and far between. Oftentimes, he was working in a studio doing portrait photos for personnel to submit with their promotion consideration. A lot of his work was documentation. Once, he went around a small base for three days photographing every building there for posterity.

He eventually left Yuma and went to Long Island, New York, to be the district photographer for the First Marine Corps District recruiting command. In New York, he worked in an office doing public affairs for the Marines. Once again, he did promotion photos for the Marines. However, this time he became familiar with promotion formats, styles, and requirements for all branches of service.

He later worked media coverage for Veteran's Day, among other events in New York City, as well as training events and documentation at Camp Pendleton. By those days, the photographers had gone digital. Along with videographers, Simon and others would provide a multimedia package to officials on base.

But his time stateside was coming on a hiatus. After arriving at First Marine Division, Camp Pendleton in April 2006, in August he was sent to Camp Fallujah, just outside of Fallujah, Iraq. While this was several years after the Battle for Fallujah, he was tasked with photographing a variety of things, including the Iraqi military, police, and government. He and others would also document and record the recruitment of Iraqi police officers. And they would go into the city to perimeter search missions or attend targeted raids.

Simon recalls a time when the Iraqi military was going into a mosque in 2006. American forces wanted proof that American troops were providing security, but not entering the mosque due to political or religious issues. Simon and others documented the events but did not enter with Iraqi forces.

His time on Camp Fallujah was not without its unique dangers. Even though he was a photographer, Simon was armed and a potential target to threatening forces. The camp would often receive indirect fire, or even mortars lobbed directly at them, daily. Nightfall was not very different, aside from everything going pitch dark. If he extended his hand, he wouldn't even be able to make out his fingers in the darkness. This always added a layer of uncertainty to already hazardous conditions.

And these hazardous conditions were perilous. Every time you left Camp Fallujah, wherever you were, you did something they called the sniper shuffle. The idea was that whenever you were in a stable area, you had to keep moving.

Maybe in a square, maybe in a triangle, or some other more irregular shape. The point was to avoid becoming an easy target for potential snipers.

Through all this, armed with an M-16, M-4, or even a pistol, Simon was also brandishing his camera. His primary mission was to be a photographer and to photograph up until the very last minute. Then, if he had to, he would return fire. Fortunately for him, he was never in a situation where he had to engage the enemy.

Simon's retirement from the military was rather sudden. After fifteen years as a Marine, he was still an E-6, a Staff Sergeant, and promotions were becoming incredibly difficult. From around 2006 to 2008, the military surged due to the Conflict in Iraq. The Marine Corps was usually staffed with one hundred seventy-five thousand active-duty Marines. That number swelled to well over two hundred thousand during the surge. The military had hoped to maintain that number, but sooner or later there came some downsizing. This time, numbers would plummet closer to the original one hundred seventy-five thousand.

But they couldn't simply kick people out, so they had to get creative thinking of ways to get people out of the Marine Corps. If you had conduct issues, you were out. If you were overweight, you were out. If you couldn't perform on the physical fitness test, you were out. Then later, when it came time for reenlistments, it became very difficult to do so.

Finally, the Marine Corps started offering those with fifteen years of service full retirements, without having to complete the full twenty years usually required. It would be at a lower pay rate, but you would keep all the benefits of insurance, exchanges, military bases, and the like. In 2014, Simon and his wife decided that it would be best for their family of six if he retired then.

Securing the Middle East

Noah Yarbrough was eighteen when the 9/11 terrorist attacks occurred. Although he had already started college, he decided that enlisting was his duty. He needed to do his part for his country. It seemed like the quickest impact he as an individual could make in the long run.

When he enlisted in the U.S. Air Force in July of 2004, he was so eager to serve that his job was immaterial. He told the recruiter that he simply wanted to choose whatever role would get him to work the fastest. This landed him in security forces, basically the Air Force police.

He completed basic training that August and then attended the police academy until January of 2005. He was later assigned to Hill Air Force Base where he would spend nearly his entire active-duty career.

Yarbrough had joined at a time when the tempo was high due to the multiple wars American forces were fighting in. He hit the ground running and deployed to the Middle East right away to support the mission. He went on to deploy there again six times in his career, and once in Japan as well.

His most difficult deployment was his third, in Basra, Iraq. For almost a year, he experienced a lot of uncertainty, long hours, and many different things that will stick with him for the rest of his life. He couldn't even call home, and seeing his friends go home with injuries or mental illness was tough to handle. He was right in the mix of the conflict, seeing his friends go home with life-changing injuries. It was hard to reconcile that those he saw today might not make it to tomorrow.

In Iraq and Afghanistan, Yarbrough largely dealt with detainees as military police. However, he didn't treat them as simply prisoners. Whether or not they liked him or whatever the circumstances of their crimes, he made the effort to get to know them for who they were, not for what they did. Even though he knew they had done wrong, he chose to give them a different image of what an American soldier could be.

He tried to sympathize, to understand. At the end of the day, some of them were decent people. They were just caught up in the conflict around them, doing what they were told to support and protect themselves and their families. Many of them hardly knew what they were doing. However, there were also detainees who despised him, Americans, and everything the United States stands for. He had to take his duties at Camp Bucca day by day. Some days were just better than others.

On his later deployment to Okinawa, Japan in 2017, he supported the local Air Force wing at Kadena Air Base and set up some supply chains. He was activated for the three years to support the deployment missions out that way. Yarbrough and others also set up the F-35 supply logistics program. It was the first theater security package for the brand-new F-35 aircraft. They mobilized twenty aircraft in the Pacific region. Yarbrough's team there won Team of the Year, and as a supervisor, he earned the title of 2017 Non-Commissioned Officer of the Year. After this colorful career in the Army, he later left active-duty service in 2018.

Farming to Arming

Rick Rother grew up on a farm just two miles south of the Prairie Island Nuclear Generating Plant. Back in 2000, farming was not the most profitable career, but he didn't have much direction besides working on the farm. And as the oldest of four kids, he had been warned that they might have trouble supporting him in pursuing a college education.

A high school friend of his suggested they go and talk to a local recruiter for the U.S. Navy. Rother then became interested in enlisting as an Aerographer's Mate, basically a meteorologist. However, the recruiter offered him the nuclear exam and Rother ended up scoring very high. The recruiter recommended he look at working on submarines with the nuclear program. So, Rother signed up for the Navy Nuclear Program and after boot camp in Great Lakes, Illinois was sent to school in Charleston, South Carolina.

Charleston was a great place, a fun place for a young eighteen-year-old to explore. He went through all his in-classroom schooling there, learning how to be a Navy Machinist Mate. He then went to Navy Nuclear Power School learning things such as nuclear physics, metallurgy, thermodynamics, and nuclear reactor technology.

After finishing his classroom training, he went to Saratoga Springs, New York to have hands-on training with Navy nuclear prototypes in the reactor plant. His last phase of training in Saratoga Springs was to learn how to become an Engineering Laboratory Technician, where he learned how to maintain the chemistry of the reactor plant and radiological controls.

After finishing his training, he received orders to meet the deployed submarine USS Memphis out of a port in Bahrain. He recalls having no idea what to pack and no contacts to guide him. Luckily, a roommate in his barracks still had a list of what to pack in his sea bag. He flew into Bahrain and landed late at night. He remembers getting off the plane and stepping directly onto the runway. He looked up and two men had machine guns trained on him. What had he gotten himself into? When he finally met the boat, he spent his first Christmas and New Year's Eve away from home while on his deployment. Christmas in Italy and New Year's in Rota, Spain.

Both submarines that Rother served on were attack submarines. The USS Memphis, which has since been decommissioned, was an old 688 class with fairwater planes. His second sub, later in his career, was the USS Virginia, the first of the newer Virginia class. The Virginia-class being one of the United States Navy's latest submarine models. There was a vast advancement in technology between the Memphis and the Virginia, and with this came a bit of a learning curve between those two submarines.

Going from farm life to submarine life wasn't easy. Rother admits to being quite homesick on his first deployment but explains that the rigor of his schedule didn't allow him to get down for too long. On the boat, he was working hard trying to qualify and standing watch. In fact, he felt some similarities to his time on the farm. Back home, he would be up at five in the morning to milk cows and might continue working from that point up until eleven at night or even midnight. It was similar hours and a comparable amount of work as a Machinist's Mate on the submarine.

Rother stood watch in the engine room of the nuclear plant, operating pumps and turning valves. He was also part of the Reactor Laboratory Division that maintained the chemistry of the nuclear reactor. They also performed radiological surveys ensuring the safety of the up to one hundred fifty crew members on board.

In addition to his time on submarines, he had several years doing shore duty. One particularly memorable three-year shore duty later inspired him to work in quality assurance. He worked at Submarine Development Squadron 12 as a Chemistry and Radiological Control Assistant. In that position, he would ensure eight submarines were ready for their Operational Reactor Safety Examination. Naval Reactors would come down once a year to do a full scrub of the boat and give the boat a rating on how well it was operating. Rother and others would go down before Naval Reactors to make sure that the boat was ready for examination. He supported a full audit of the Engineering Department and focus on chemistry and radiological surveys that Reactor Laboratory Division performed.

It was quite the journey, his twelve years in the military. Rother considers himself fortunate to have gotten to experience all that he did in the Navy. He traveled to Bahrain, Dubai, France, Gibraltar, Israel, Italy, Norway, Scotland, and Spain during his time in the service. He even keeps a vial of water from the North Pole where he went underneath the ice cap in 2005. To him, many great things came out of being in the military and on submarines, things you would never expect from a farm kid.

Going Nuclear

When Joe Tolbert was a year into his college education, he didn't see it playing out into getting a job. At the time, he happened to see a U.S. Navy nuclear operator ad in the paper, talking about how much money you could make there. So, he went down and took the test, and they were impressed with his scores. A few months later, he was going to Great Lakes boot camp and heading to Nuclear Power School.

It was intense initially because he had to be in the top ten percent. They chose him to be an electrician as he had been in the top ten percent of his electricity mate class. When he got to Orlando, where the program was based at the time, he only had to maintain a decent grade point average. He started out studying about thirty hours a week, but before the program was over, he was up to sixty hours a week just to maintain his 3.2 grade point average through the program.

After Electrical Power School, he volunteered for submarines and ended up on fast attack submarines out of Norfolk, Virginia doing electrical work. He also ran the reactors on board. It was a shock to his system because he had never been on submarines before. But after an adjustment period, he was on subs his entire Navy career.

Back then, he and others on board basically lived eighteen-hour days with a six-hour watch. For another six-hour block, they did maintenance or leisure activities. This left them with six hours of sleep. The Navy has since changed this schedule because they figured out it wasn't healthy.

He hadn't planned on it, but he ended up retiring from the Navy in 2000 after twenty years. During those years, he had served on four different submarines and done tours on a submarine support vessel and as an instructor. In the end, he was a First-Class Electrician Mate with a Bachelor's in applied engineering, paid for by the Navy.

Alaska Calling

After graduating high school in 1991, Brad Vander Plas joined the Iowa National Guard. He was influenced by his older brother, who had joined the Army National Guard earlier. His brotherly advice was for Vander Plas to make a little bit of money serving his country, perhaps get a college education paid for. Another family influence was their father, who had been in the National Guard as well. His unit was even activated to participate in the Vietnam War towards the end of the conflict.

In the National Guard, Vander Plas went to drills one weekend out of each month, which helped a lot once he got to basic training. At that point, he already knew how to wear the uniform and polish his boots. And he now already knew the orders of the higher ranking. The sergeants and officers he got to know taught him many things, helping him with familiarizing himself. All this knowledge was incredibly useful. Instead of coming into basic blind, as many do when they first come into basic training, he could stay focused on working towards his goals.

He joined the Army as an infantry mortar operator. His location options for his station were either Alaska or Korea. Well, he wasn't ready for a foreign country, so he picked Alaska. Even though it was technically a domestic move, he remembers receiving a bundle of vaccines like he was on his way to the jungle somewhere.

But what was he doing with mortars in Alaska? Well, the Alaskan border is a globally strategic foothold. From World War II, American forces were first shipping planes over to Russia from Alaskan peninsulas. The Japanese even invaded a part of Alaska in 1943 during the Battle of Attu.

The mortar Vander Plas used was a 4.2-inch mortar, nicknamed the four-deuce. Most of the time they were used in the back of armored vehicles. But as the four-deuce mortar is big and heavy, it has since been replaced by 120mm mortars, which are lighter and easier to maintain. These mortars are still used today, mostly in tracked vehicles. However, mortars are primarily used to suppress opposing troops and allow infantry and armored units to move into strategic positions. 81mm and 60mm mortars are used in light Infantry units.

He spent 1993 to 1996 at Fort Wainwright, Alaska, where he also met and married his wife. When he reenlisted, he was transferred to Fort Carson, Colorado. They kind of liked the area there, but it was very busy. Meanwhile, his unit was constantly training in the field, so he was away from home a lot. After a little over two years in Colorado, he reenlisted again, and Fort Wainwright came up again. At that time, he didn't have much love for Alaska. Both he and his wife were ready to get out of there. But he thought, why not go back for a bit? In 1998, he was set to leave Colorado.

Unfortunately, just before his move back to Fort Wainwright, Vander Plas was playing football for physical training and landed flat on his back. This triggered a terrible pain and muscle spasms among other symptoms for the next several years. During the next two years of his enlistment, he was offered to reclassify into another Military Occupational Specialty, but he was fed up with the whole situation and decided to leave the military.

When he first got out, he was given a ten-percent disability rating. He was directed to the Fairbanks Vet Center, and they did a fantastic job. They helped him get his records together and get back into civilian life. And they thought that he had not received a high enough disability rating. So, they helped him get a physical with the VA doctors in Anchorage to look at everything again. They came back and recommended a thirty-percent disability rating and he accepted.

Overseas Support

Milt Buker grew up in a little town in the northeastern corner of Utah. His family had a farm, and he worked on the farm every day keeping animals and showing horses. He had decided to become a veterinarian. After one year in college, it was apparent that he would not have enough money to complete all the schooling to become a veterinarian. His family convinced him to join the Army, following in his grandfather's footsteps.

Buker loved his time in the Army. He supported special forces operations, traveling all over the world on constant deployments. He supported activities in Afghanistan, Haiti, Honduras, and Somalia. This support included everything from assisting after natural disasters to helping people get access to food and medical supplies. He was never bored, and every mission was unique. His only disappointment is that many never understood what they were trying to do. Negative spins from the regime made delivery of aid difficult to get to those truly in need. Oftentimes, he would be unsure if someone was friend or foe. He even reflects that sometimes they could have been both to an extent.

During his time serving in overseas, he was building helipads to support missions in Kosovo, Macedonia, and Bosnia. He was training a new soldier on how to operate an armored bulldozer with mine protection when the operator accidentally hit the hydraulic release. The front blade dropped onto a piece of pipe causing it to swing up and hit him across the back, fracturing his lower back. Military service is rough on the body. Buker suffered injuries to his back, both ankles, knee, hands, and has hearing loss. Despite this, he maintains that he has no regrets about his service. After his injury, he left the military. But he reflects that if he not been injured, he likely would have stayed until retirement.

Seeing the World of Energy

Kevin Hernandez always knew he wanted to serve in the military at some point in his life. While not part of a military family, he had grown up surrounded by friends who were veterans. Their influence had instilled in him a sense of service.

As he was finishing his undergraduate degree in anthropology at the University of Tennessee, he knew that if he didn't join then, he wouldn't again have the chance to go back and do it. It would be very hard to start a career and then go back and serve. And so, he seized on the opportunity and made the decision then to join the United States Navy.

The Navy mantra "Join the navy and see the world!" had appealed to him, and that's just what he did, serving for eight years on two different sea duty assignments. One a guided missile destroyer out of Norfolk, Virginia and the other a minesweeper out of Manama, Bahrain.

Minesweepers, Hernandez says, is as old school as you can get. Going from an Aegis destroyer where everything is computerized or digital, to a minesweeper which is a wooden hull dragging cables behind the ship, was quite the change. It's the same technology developed in World War II. It was a little nerve wracking at times, but exciting. Small crews and small ships brought more responsibility.

2002 to 2003 was a tough time to be in the Northern Persian Gulf, but it was an exciting and rewarding assignment. When he came back to the United States, he spent some time in Washington D.C., which is where he got bit by the energy bug.

When he was still in the Navy, he supported Congress as a liaison, mostly advocating for the Navy positions, but also providing logistical support to Congress. It was a lot of international travel. Soon after leaving Bahrain, he was back overseas leading congressional delegations to Iraq and Afghanistan, liaising with the State Department, foreign governments, and others. When he eventually left the Navy after several years, he stayed on the Hill working on military and veteran's policy in the Senate.

At that point, many of the major issues in national security were concerned with oil. Energy policy was focused on the amount of oil the country was importing at the time. There was a lot of talk in national security circles on how to break our dependency on international sources of oil for our energy. That's what piqued Hernandez's interest.

He started on the oil and gas side, but quickly moved into the energy and electricity side. He went back to school, got his MBA from Duke, and joined ScottMadden, drawn to the firm's reputation in energy.

Military to Military Spouse

When she first enlisted in the Army, Stephanie Roper's primary Military Occupational Specialty (MOS) was as a Military Records Specialist in Human Resources, a familiar field. Her mother had spent most of her career in HR for a major U.S. based retail company. Roper, like her mother, loved connecting and interacting with people and HR felt like a natural fit.

She worked in that role for her first two years, and then got an opportunity to transition into a new role in a secondary MOS as either a Chaplain's Assistant or a Legal Specialist in the JAG Corp. She had always been fascinated by religion and the motivations behind people's beliefs. Having grown up as a Catholic and enjoying learning about religion, the role of a Chaplain's Assistant sounded like a great fit as well. But the Chaplain that she would be assigned to assist spoke Latin, a language that she would have had to learn in order to be his assistant. So, she decided to go the legal route and became a Legal Specialist. And she absolutely loved it.

As a Legal Specialist, Roper supervised duties associated with court-martial proceedings, line of duty investigations, board proceedings, and claim investigations. She also specialized in EEO Affairs, Sexual Harassment Compliance, Armed Services Code of Conduct, and Family Preparedness Planning.

Roper initially entered into what is referred to as a six by two contract. The agreement required that she be in the Army Reserves for eight years, drilling once a month for the first six years. The final two years, she would be on reserve in the event she needed to be activated for deployment, etc.

After basic training and Advanced Individual Training, she returned to Austin, Texas and began her first semester as a college student. Unfortunately, she had missed the beginning of her first semester at Texas A&M, so she went to a local college in Austin, because she could participate in later registration, and planned to transfer to Texas A&M the following year.

A few years later, Roper was a typical college student who also served in the Army Reserve. Soon, she began thinking about going from "Green to Gold" by transitioning to full time service as an Officer Candidate and making a career out of the military. However, between 1991 and 1999, post-Desert Storm during the Clinton Administration, the government began downsizing the military. Military installations were closing all over the country. Roper was uneasy about this and soon found herself shifting gears. She eventually married Rick Roper, thus becoming a military spouse, a completely different trajectory and a complicated path going forward.

Supplied Success

Growing up in southern Florida, Miranda Penn was always very studious. She loved school and learning, and she knew that she was going to go to college. Her family couldn't necessarily pay for her to go to college, but that was still the expectation set for her. In fact, she was accepted at Southern University in Louisiana.

But during her senior year of high school, an Army recruiter got to her. He talked to her about traveling and getting college paid for, and Penn had stars in her eyes. She wasn't sure if she wanted to go straight to college anymore, and if the military would pay for it later, it was a win-win. She sat her family down and broke the news that she was not going to college, she was joining the Army.

The first two weeks of basic training were rough. The physical training was grueling, and the drill sergeants yelling in her face didn't make things any easier. She even thought she might have made the wrong decision at first. But after the first week or two, she adjusted. She came to know what was expected of her and learned to go with the flow and do what she needed to do.

After eight weeks of basic, she was sent to Virginia for Advanced Individual Training, where she learned her trade as a 92 Alpha, an Automated Logistical Supply Specialist. She and others managed all aspects of the warehouse, processing, and ordering parts for all the field artillery at Fort Sill, Oklahoma. Much like supply chain work, she explains.

She enjoyed the work and spent all four of years of her service at Fort Sill. She was fortunate to stay in her position and go to school at night. Later, when she left the service, many of her friends who stayed in were deployed nonstop in the wake of 9/11.

Pictured: Cassandra Wheeler (top left), Josh King (top right, right), Jesse Lockhart (center left, right), Chad Craven (center right), Brian Carlson (bottom left), Bill Krieger (bottom right)

Pictured: Joe Tolbert (top left), Jeff Ihnen (top center), Mike Rich (top right), Stephanie Roper (center left), Chad Craven (center right), Kersha Brown (bottom)

Pictured: Stephanie Roper (top, far right), Ron Wild (center left, left), Sophia Eccleston (center right), Rick Rother (bottom, right)

CHAPTER THREE

Veterans in Transition to the Utilities Industry

Learning and Unlearning

The transition from Soldier, Sailor, Marine, Airman, or Coast Guardsman to civilian is oftentimes fairly smooth. But at least as often it is not. There are so many differences between the military and civilian workplace to learn and many habits acquired while in uniform to unlearn.

To really understand where the veteran working alongside you at your utility, agency, association or firm is coming from, you must appreciate the trials of this transition. How the vet adjusts to less clarity about the organization's mission and its chain of command. How the vet comes to appreciate the less intense comradery of civilian workplaces. And adopts the art of managing his or her own career. And also leaves behind, as much as is possible, the pleasant and not at all pleasant memories of deployments.

In this chapter, we visit with a few of the veterans in the energy and utilities industry and focus on their step into one world from another. Starting with Air Force vet Noah Yarbrough who can now be found at PacifiCorp.

Distribution, Sure, But of What?

Noah Yarbrough, now a manager of procurement and materials at PacifiCorp, left the U.S. Air Force in June of 2014 after ten years of active duty. Though he has remained in the Air Force Reserves and has been nearly as active in military service since, in assignments such as helping to develop the supply chain for the F-35 Lightning II stealth fighter both domestically and at Kadena Air Base in Japan.

This transition to a civilian, albeit one with a continuing involvement in our national defense, was a definite change of lifestyle. In the service, there are stable expectations. So, for Yarbrough, making the decision to leave active duty was hard. To prepare, he started school several years before, receiving his bachelor's in criminal justice in 2015, and then his master's in transportation and logistics in 2017.

And he threw himself into civilian life. Learning how to deal with others outside of the military was different to say the least. Once he had gotten used to it, after a couple of years, he secured a job at the Defense Logistics Agency, as a material skills technician.

A couple of years later, in 2018, Rocky Mountain Power, a subsidiary of PacifiCorp, which is in turn a subsidiary of Berkshire Hathaway Energy, happened to have some distribution manager spots open. Yarbrough naturally applied given his experience in logistics, in other words, managing the distribution of parts and equipment.

Little did he realize that Rocky Mountain was looking for power distribution managers, that is, managing the distribution of electric power, not of parts and equipment. Yarbrough did make it through the first round of interviews. But then he explained to a secretary there that he had no experience in the power industry, let alone managing the distribution of power.

Nevertheless, Rocky Mountain liked him. So, he made it through the second and third rounds of interviews and ended up receiving an offer, to work as an assistant manager in (power) distribution. After a year, in the summer of 2019, he was able to switch to a more familiar logistics role at the company.

Looking back on the experience, Yarbrough feels like he has had a relatively smooth transition from airman to civilian. He attributes much of this to his upbringing. He's a people person who was raised never to pass judgment on anybody until he got to know them. So, he approached his transition and coming into the utilities industry with an open mind and did his best to be receptive to change.

But there were still habits to unlearn. In the service, when someone has a higher rank than you, you do what they say regardless. Coming to the civilian workforce as a manager, he fought with himself sometimes when he told an employee to do something, and it took them a bit of time.

He kept reminding himself that not everyone has come from the same world that he has. Yarbrough adjusted his management style and has worked to be as approachable as possible.

Even so, Yarbrough misses many aspects of his military service, the first being its comradery. When you're put under stress, living for someone else, fighting for someone else, and you see all these different personalities come together for one cause, that's bigger than everybody else. He built some strong relationships that he will have for the rest of his life.

To him, one of the biggest differences out in the civilian world is that in the military, you see many of those that you work with at their worst, their saddest, when they have nothing left. Even in the face of this adversity, they rise up, put their life on the line, and strive to do good by their country. You really get to see the inner workings of somebody and build a lot of trust.

Private Eye

Ron Wild came to work for Rocky Mountain Power in the summer of 2013 after being recruited to join the company's customer service team at the Casper, Wyoming service center. As a regional business manager, as he sees it, he works for everyone in Wyoming, supporting large industrials, communities, non-profits, and government to make tomorrow better than yesterday.

But when Wild left the U.S. Air Force at the end of 1992, after ten years as a security specialist, he really didn't know what he was going to do. He had no plan.

He was required to go over to the Veterans Administration due to a neck injury he sustained in the service. When he went there, as part of his out-processing, they gave him an aptitude test and offered to send him to school for anything he wanted.

At twenty-eight years old, Wild was asking himself, what do I want to be when I grow up? And he didn't know. The first three suggestions from the test came back: police officer, military officer, private investigator.

He decided to become a private eye and remembers it as a lot of fun. Back in the day, investigators were using big VHS video cameras. One time, he walked into a bar with a camera, set it up on the booth behind him, and videotaped a man chatting up his girlfriend. The man's wife had hired Wild to find out if her husband was cheating on her. The husband hardly paid attention to Wild and was caught red-handed.

While private investigator work was fun, it didn't pay well. With a disabled wife, a teenage daughter, and a preschool age son, he knew he needed to make a change.

He couldn't go back into the military due to his injury. For the same reason, he didn't think it was wise to work in law enforcement. And he didn't feel like he had the personality for politics, another possibility. So where did that leave him? Engineering.

Engineering seemed like a good path. The VA asked Wild what kind of engineering he wanted to do. He had no idea.

So, he went over to the Cheyenne Public Library and found a book on engineers. He started looking through it and came across a picture of two guys with a computer. Wild liked computers. He'd had a computer since he was eighteen, back when you had to program everything in the software language BASIC.

At the top of the page in that book were the words electrical engineer. So, he returned to the VA and told them that was what he wanted to be.

He started at Laramie County Community College in 1994, nearly two years after leaving the Air Force, and received his associate degree in mathematics in three years. While he was there, he was even president of the honors society and a member of the calculus team. Quite a change for the former private eye.

After graduating Laramie County, he went on to the University of Wyoming, where he earned his bachelor's in electrical engineering two years later, in 1999. He even managed the power lab of the electrical engineering department.

Soon after graduation, Wild went to work for a carbon fibers technology company, where he stayed for a dozen years. Starting as an electrical engineer he eventually became a quality, safety, environmental and IT manager, and then operations support manager (reporting directly to the Evanston, Wyoming facility's general manager). He simultaneously began teaching math at Western Wyoming Community College as adjunct faculty and became the chair of his county's economic development commission, as well as its community emergency response team.

In 2008, Wild's son graduated high school and joined the U.S. Marine Corps. Because searching daily for your son's name on the war zone's casualty list is not conducive to a good mental state, Wild went back to school full-time to distract himself. He received his master's in business leadership within two years.

Wild finally entered the utilities industry in 2013. One of Rocky Mountain's customer service teams was looking for a replacement for another individual who had left. Wild already knew most of the people on the team through his many activities in the state. The team reached out and encouraged him to put in an application. Before long, they called Wild and offered him the job.

Major to Uber Driver

Tom Rollins advanced through the ranks to U.S. Army Lieutenant and to Captain between 2007, when he received his bachelor's in computer science and completed the Reserve Officer Training Corps program, and 2013, when he became assistant operations officer for four companies of around five hundred soldiers at Fort Stewart, Georgia.

Along the way he served as a communications platoon leader in Iraq and conducted numerous combat patrols with and without Iraqi military and police forces. And he toured Afghanistan as well. Rollins sustained a litany of injuries during these deployments and combat training with an accumulating effect.

Rollins was then made commander for a communications company of fifty-two soldiers at Fort Stewart in 2014. Afterwards he spent almost four years at that critical center for the nation's communications defense, the National Security Agency at Fort Meade, Maryland, and finally retired as a Major in February of 2019.

At that point in his Army career, he knew what he was good at, and what he wanted to do. His assignment was more ambiguous than what he was looking for. He had two boys living with their mother in a different state. And as an officer going forward, he would be moving around quite often, and with little support from the military for the areas he was interested in. Though, Rollins says, if the Army would have given him a position and unit that aligned with his passion and training, he likely would have stayed in.

He applied to a veteran transition support program, through some connections his wife had, and was accepted. This special program would fill the gaps in the military transition assistance program.

They flew him out to one of their flagship locations where he went to a three-day boot camp. They instructed Rollins on everything from how to elevator pitch himself, to resume writing, to interviewing. He went to the program full of confidence. But on the first day his resume evaluation went differently than he had imagined. He was working with one veteran and one civilian from the program's faculty, both with a decade of experience. One of them looked at Rollins and warned, now, before you open this, I just want you to understand that this was a great first cut and we've got a great base here. When they opened the folder, it looked like a red pen had blown up on it. Rollins was shocked.

Regardless, he remembers the whole transition as amazing. The group and the opportunities they provided him put him in a great position to move forward. He followed his wife to Florida and transitioned into the Army Reserves. His backup plan was to Active Guard Reserve if he couldn't find a job. But he was sure he would find a job.

During the first ninety days in Florida, he went from a senior Army officer to driving an Uber, getting yelled at by rich people for not opening their door right. But he was raised by his father and grandfather to be a doer. His father always told him, it doesn't matter what you know or who you know, if you can't deliver, then you're not useful and you will not be successful.

He found himself in Florida realizing he didn't know anybody. And he, actually, didn't know how to get a job.

His father-in-law was retired Navy. So, he empathized. Rollins reached out to him, and his father-in-law started introducing him to people that he knew in the community.

Next thing Rollins knew, through a friend of a friend of a client, he got invited to a Miami Dolphins game. And it was in a box. There, he met some young gentlemen who were part of the IT company who owned the box.

Throughout the course of the game, he found out that the CEO and the CFO were Army veterans. Rollins shared his story with them, and the CEO offered him a job. He wouldn't be able to serve in the role for long and would only be paid around forty percent of what he was making previously, but it would help him get on his feet. That was a lucky break, and it taught Rollins that maybe it was about who you know.

While he had this transition job, he left his resume at several contingent worker program firms in South Florida, trying to get a more permanent position. Meanwhile, he exercised his post-9/11 G.I. Bill and was accepted at Northwestern University's yellow ribbon program to earn his master's in information systems security in 2019.

One of the contingent worker program companies floated his resume and called him. They explained that Florida Power & Light had a job opening at a help desk. While his capabilities were way above this role, they said, this was the type of company where, if he could get a foot in the door, he could figure out the rest.

Rollins was on board. And luck was on his side. He got a call about three weeks later from a manager in cybersecurity. Florida Power & Light needed a program manager to create an insider threat program. Rollins said he could do it, though he didn't really know what that meant. They scheduled an interview in Miami. For the next week, Rollins went into research mode.

The only social media account he had at the time was LinkedIn. He started doing some open-source research there. He sent a message to every single person he could find that had testified in a congressional hearing for an insider threat case over the past ten years.

It was a move outside of his comfort zone. But he did need information. In his messages, he introduced himself and asked if they had any advice on building a new insider threat program. A lot of these people that had testified as experts in this space either worked for or owned a company that charged people to do this. To his surprise, every single one of them scheduled a call with him.

Armed with all this new knowledge, he later got the job, set up Florida Power & Light's insider threat program, and at first, ran the program by himself. Now, he manages an enterprise-wide program focused on cyber threat identification and risk reduction. Of the fifteen in this group that he leads, eight of them are military veterans.

Home Depot Moment

When Mike Rich returned home in September of 2005, from a U.S. Army deployment in Iraq, he went straight back to his day job at Home Depot, where he had started in 1997. Although, he returned as a department manager. He hasn't been deployed again since, even throughout the several campaigns that have occurred over the years.

Within a week or two of coming back from that deployment, he was in the aisles of Home Depot trying to help customers. Rich was grateful for that return to normalcy, in a way. But he really struggled with people's priorities.

For instance, one day there was a difficult customer in the faucet aisle searching for a part. The man was vocally upset. Rich finally turned to him and said,

> Hey, look. You know what? I just returned from a deployment two weeks ago. I was in Iraq. And I understand that you're upset about this part. But look, nobody's shooting at you. It's not that serious. We have avenues to get to the part and let me try to help you with that.

The man was taken aback at that point. He thanked Rich for his service and came back later for his part. It was a moment dedicated to changing perspectives.

Rich believes that his time in the Army has absolutely helped him in his civilian career. The sheer variety and number of experiences that he's gained being in the military has brought a wealth of knowledge that he brings to his civilian side every day. The variety of people you encounter in the military is incredibly diverse. Different personalities and backgrounds abound. These experiences helped him learn how to better work with people, to communicate and relate.

Coming into a corporate environment, these skills help him do his job. He can raise issues when they need to be addressed and remove obstacles in support of the mission. He sees his diverse experience as key to his success, to understanding where others are coming from and how to value that diversity in his workplace.

He continues to serve in the Army Reserve to this day. Over the course of his eighteen-year career, he has since converted to an officer role as Captain Supply Officer in Trenton, New Jersey.

However, he has simultaneously focused on his civilian career in the corporate environment of American Water, where he is now director for corporate procurement and national categories at its Camden, New Jersey offices. He joined American Water in February of 2017.

Though this wasn't his first position in the utilities industry. Years earlier, he had become a supply chain representative at Arizona Public Service, in 2007. And Rich then began an eight-year career in which he was promoted a few times, ultimately to a program manager leader for the supply chain strategic initiatives department. In those first couple of years at Arizona Public Service, he also completed his bachelor's in global business from Arizona State University.

When he came back from Iraq, his biggest challenge in the transition was re-grounding himself in his old, yet newly unfamiliar environment. It was more about balance than anything else. He must juggle his responsibilities at American Water, as a husband, as a father of two, and then ultimately to the military.

There have even been times where he had to take off work to go do work for the Army. He also has training and drill days. These sometimes occur during the work week, even though his usual duty dates are on the weekends.

He constantly reminds his military supervisors that anything they get from him during the week is above and beyond. His full-time commitment is to American Water.

They help him to provide for himself and family. But really, everybody in his life must be flexible.

Rich says the one person in his life that deals with it the most is his wife, who supports him in both of his careers. While he is grateful to have her support, he is very much looking forward to hitting his twenty years in the Reserves and his subsequent retirement from the military as soon as possible.

His kids are getting older, playing sports, and he wants to dedicate more time to being their father. So, for Rich, it's not so much the transition into corporate as much as how he balances it.

Amazon Fulfillment Center

During Josh King's last four years in the U.S. Navy, through June of 2006, he taught ROTC at Villanova University. He remembers it as easily his most favorite job during his time in the military. He was the face of the Navy on campus. Meanwhile, while he was teaching, he was also learning. He earned his master's in business administration from Villanova, also in 2006, compliments of the Navy once again.

The Navy really set him up for success. Though his transition wasn't without its difficulties. At the time, there wasn't a push to hire veterans the way there is right now.

To secure a job, King worked with headhunters whose focus was placing former military, the junior officers particularly, into civilian positions. Of course, he applied to numerous places online as well. But he got zero leads. The companies working with those headhunters were the ones that truly saw the benefits of hiring military officers.

King was jobless for a few months. He finally joined Amazon as an area manager in one of their fulfillment centers. He worked in that role for about six months. It just wasn't a good fit. In fact, he describes his time working there as pretty crazy.

So, he gave up on trying to stay in his hometown of Philadelphia and resolved that he would move if a good job was available. He joined a small startup out of Boston in April of 2007, PowerAdvocate, that focused on supply chain for utilities. Its CEO was a West Point graduate and King's direct supervisor was a former submarine officer. They were specifically hunting for submarine officers with an MBA. King was a perfect fit.

Consulting was great for King. Working with such a variety of clients, solving a variety of different problems, was a lot of fun. It also helped him to identify his strengths and what roles he thrived in. He also got to travel even more than he had in the military. He admits though that the travel lost its allure after three years of spending a hundred fifty nights a year in hotels and living on airplanes. Which is when, in May of 2010, he took a position with Arizona Public Service as a manager for strategic procurement.

The aforementioned Mike Rich had been at Arizona Public Service for three years in its supply function as well. They worked together there through November of 2016 and they both moved to American Water and its supply function in Camden within months of each other.

Vet's Resume

At the end of 2013, Ramon Mitchell allowed his active-duty contract to expire and transitioned to a reservist position within Washington State's Army National Guard. He maintained his combat engineer occupation, serving in that capacity stateside and in Afghanistan, though he mainly performed emergency response in the state of Washington, engaging in wildland firefighting.

Every year he would be sent out to dig trenches for fire breaks, hose down evacuated houses, or man checkpoints on roads in and out of fire zones. Even facing fire was less stressful than combat, because as a guard they weren't in the thick of the fire, rather supporting the professional firefighters.

When he later applied for jobs, he continually got rejected. People looked at his resume, and they saw someone with a two-year Master's of Business Administration, from the University of Portland, but they also saw a six-year gap between receiving that degree and when he received his undergrad degree in economics from Reed College.

Of course, he had the generic Army items on there: the values of his service, integrity, and personal development. But what else could he say? He knew how to operate a machine gun, and how to drive combat vehicles. That wasn't going to do him much good in an office environment. It was difficult to express to employers what skills he could bring to the table. He had a heightened attention to detail and the ability to think clearly and to divorce himself from his emotions in a high stress or high impact environment. Yet he couldn't necessarily demonstrate those skills, at least not in a corporate manner.

In the summer of 2015, while Mitchell was still a reservist, he finally got a job offer, from PacifiCorp, working at the Portland, Oregon headquarters. But it was a low-ball offer. He was making a buck intern salary with a master's degree.

He started off in a data analytics role, supporting the development of customers' electricity rates, within the regulatory department. It was just the start he needed. Mitchell proved himself, still using those values and strengths picked up in the Army. He moved on to performing data analytics and policy development for regional energy markets, supporting least-cost solutions for serving customers' electricity, within the energy supply department.

He gained respect over time as someone who was always focused and able to get the job done. His attention to detail, ability to work under time pressure, and discipline allowed him to rapidly increase his salary up to the level of his peers within three short years. At that point, at the end of 2016, he chose to leave the Army National Guard.

While at PacifiCorp, Mitchell served as program manager for the Western Energy Imbalance Market within the transmission grid operations department. His goal was to ensure reliable service for electric customers as it relates to the Western EIM. These days, he is working at Portland General Electric as Senior Trading Analyst, staying involved in the Energy Imbalance Market.

Chuck E. Cheese

After six years in the U.S. Marine Corps as an aviation radio technician, Brian Carlson left the military in the summer of 1998. He had initially planned to reenlist. But he decided against it due to marital disagreements with his now ex-wife. Looking back, he says he kind of wishes he had stayed with the Marines. But when he did get out, he didn't know what to do. So, he went back home to his family.

Many in Carlson's family had worked as plumbers their whole lives. He therefore helped out working plumbing jobs for a while until he could figure out what to do.

He eventually answered an ad in the newspaper for a technical person to set up equipment. The description was very vague. He came to find out the job entailed installing video games and animatronics for a new Chuck E. Cheese restaurant that was being built. Once it opened, he became the technical manager and later, the owner made him general manager. He held that position for what he describes as possibly some of the worst three years of his life.

After three years, he found himself at YKK, a zipper manufacturer. He was working as a technical engineer, on machines and production. Like his work with Chuck E. Cheese, Carlson was not thrilled. The production environment's monotonous repetition was killing him.

One day, a coworker left to work at a plant for Flint Energies. Carlson asked him to call him if there was ever another opening. About a year later, he got that call. He started in March of 2003.

Finally at the co-op, he could relate his work life to his previous military experience. He missed the camaraderie of the Marine Corps, though his new position put him in another new family. It filled in what he was looking for, what he was missing from his time in the service.

Carlson started doing substation maintenance. Then, after around two years, he became a supervisor of the transformer shop.

Later, a job at the communication department opened. Carlson now heads that very department as manager of communications technology. He attributes his start in the communication department to his military service, believing his previous experience is what got his foot in the door.

He now works with fiber optics, telephone systems, microwave radio systems, two-way radios, distribution, automation, communication systems, and more. Carlson has been with Flint Energies for eighteen years. He says he's not leaving until they make him.

Jamaican Restaurant

When Kersha Brown separated from the U.S. Army in 2007, after eight years of military service as a petroleum fuel specialist, she refocused on her education to earn an associate of arts and sciences in criminal justice degree from Lehigh University. A decade later she earned her bachelor's degree in organizational leadership from Manhattan College.

But before that time at Manhattan College, Brown opened her family's Jamaican restaurant, Emmanuel's Jamaican Indian restaurant, in Harlem, together with her father. After five years, they closed the restaurant. Brown was job hunting once again.

She briefly worked as an office assistant, typing, making phone calls, and producing print outs and blueprints. She eventually found another position at Consolidated Edison, working as a meter reader, a position eventually phased out due to the advent of digital meters.

This position had its own unique difficulties, from making sure that tenants had their pets put away during readings to venturing into basements. Her biggest issues were the surprises she found in basements: cockroaches, rats, people hiding out, or even superintendent clubhouses. She had to be careful about what she found and what was going on there.

After three and a half years reading meters and then a brief year-long stint in construction management, Brown went into corporate security in 2008. Aside from day-to-day security operations at Con Edison's headquarters in New York City, she also oversees contracted guards for the New York City area facilities of Manhattan, Westchester, and the Bronx. She even combats sabotage to Con Edison's systems from a variety of sources, whether it's retaliation from disgruntled employees or other antagonists.

Soldiers to Scholars

Jesse Lockhart's military service wasn't without its sacrifices. He loved to be around his kids, play sports with his boys, and get outside in the summertime. But with the job he had, the U.S. Navy would often send him away. If a disbursing clerk got relieved on a ship, Lockhart was called in to handle the pay accounts and disbursing side of things.

He had an independent duty classification handling all the finances and accounting of a ship's disbursing office by himself. He would have to stay on that ship without a superior to supervise him, until someone was sent to replace him.

Four summers in a row, he was taken away from home. He was tired of it, fed up. But a friend told him to stick it out. Lockhart was just too close to retirement and finally did after twenty years. It turned out to be the best thing he could have done. The benefits of his Navy retirement made a significant difference in his transition from military life. It took a lot of pressure off, not worrying about things like insurance.

But what did he want to do in his new civilian life? Well, he always liked working with kids. Many of his family members were educators, so he found a new path there. He started working with the Soldiers to Scholars program, mentoring at-risk youth in the Orlando, Florida area.

He also worked for the Orange County public school system, coaching both elementary and middle school sports teams on the side. He enjoyed learning to understand these kids, being a motivator, a positive influence. His philosophy was that he couldn't stop them from doing wrong, but he could encourage them to think about their actions and the consequences they might incur. They would always have to be accountable, admit when they had done wrong, and accept the consequences of the decisions they had made.

Around 2003, Lockhart's mother was back in his hometown in Georgia battling lung issues associated with chronic obstructive pulmonary disease. He was living in Orlando at the time and originally had no intentions of working for any company in his hometown. But after discussing the situation with his wife, friends, and relatives, Lockhart knew he had to get back there. And Flint Electric Membership Corporation was hiring.

Now known as Flint Energies, the cooperative serves ninety thousand customers in central Georgia, over two-thirds of which are in Houston County. One of its customers in Chattahoochee County is a rather large one, Fort Benning.

He interviewed with both Flint Energies and the Houston County Board of Education, and then spent the weekend with his mother. The next week he was offered positions with both organizations. But Flint said he could start with them anytime, while his job with the school board wouldn't start for months. That was his sign. He accepted the job with Flint to be close to his mother.

Unfortunately, his mother ended up passing just two weeks after he started working at Flint. She was the second immediate family member to pass in a span of two years. His younger sister had passed unexpectedly the year before. The family of five was now left with three. The Lockhart's considered moving back to Florida. But Lockhart's father asked to stay in Georgia. So, they did, and Lockhart has been working with Flint Energies ever since.

He started as a member services representative working the front counters and waiting on customers. Within a year or so, he was promoted to load control database coordinator. In that role, he monitored poultry houses and irrigation loads, along with residential air conditioners, water heaters and pool pumps, ensuring they were off the grid during scheduled load management operating hours.

Working with the vendor's advanced technology for load control, Flint Energies soon realized that the technology could be used for metering. Now that technology provides input for every aspect of the cooperative, from billing, to engineering, to member support. These days, Lockhart's job title has changed. He now serves those ninety thousand customers as Flint's supervisor of communications technology.

Fish Out of Water

Miranda Penn knew after a year or two in the U.S. Army that she wasn't going to make a career out of it. She planned to finish her education instead and enter the civilian work force.

She spent part of her time in the military managing her financial situation. Penn earned both her bachelor's and master's degrees through the military, plus she paid off her car, finishing military service debt-free.

Penn then moved to Georgia, living with her aunt. In the six months after she left the military, she dedicated herself to job searching every day, applying to all the major companies in Atlanta, including Coca-Cola and the postal service.

Penn eventually landed a temp job at Georgia Power. When she could, she applied for a permanent position, and was accepted. She's been there ever since.

But the move from military to civilian work wasn't smooth, as is the case for a lot of veterans. Penn felt like a fish out of water in such a structured corporate environment. In the military, it was different. She was accustomed to communicating in a different manner. So, it took her a while to figure out the corporate culture.

In fact, it took about a year or two at the utility before she could really feel confident and comfortable. Penn was put in a position where she had to make new friends quickly, to network.

She reflects now that many veterans aren't great at networking. It isn't a skill taught during their time in the service. Rather, their focus is always accomplishing the mission. A major shift in mindset is required to succeed in a civilian environment.

Penn explains that the first job she had was, effectively, helping her colleagues to understand her and learning to understand them. She would always come to meetings early and sit alone, which led others to think she was a bit of a loner. She was simply focused on getting all the information in order to focus on the mission. It took Penn some time to switch her thought process.

These days, Penn serves as a power delivery buyer at Georgia Power. Basically, she is responsible for items that they call pole line hardware, which are essential to getting people's power turned back on. She's in a group with commodity responsibilities and material sourcing. Others in the group buy transformers, power wire and cable, and safety equipment.

Division Downsized

After twenty years of service in the U.S. Navy, Joe Tolbert's transition to civilian life was mostly an issue of picking a job that he wanted. He was already an electrician. Due to the size of the crew of the submarines he served on, he had done a lot of mechanical work as well.

Initially, he wanted to go back home, to be close to family. Tolbert's first job in Indiana was as a shift supervisor in a steel mill. Though, at that time, in 2000, the steel industry wasn't doing well. Less than a year after he took the job, his company filed for chapter 11 bankruptcy.

He later worked for Eaton Cutler-Hammer as a commissioning engineer, commissioning and repairing electrical switchgear. It was an easy transition for Tolbert, as he had already been doing maintenance work and supervising at the steel mill.

It was a great opportunity to be a field service engineer. Eaton has satellite offices in almost every state on the east coast, with some in the west as well.

The work exposed him to electrical distribution systems at utilities and commercial plants. Eaton even paid for his master's in project management.

But, after Tolbert had been working there for five years, Eaton lost its competitive edge. His division was downsized. He had built a reputation around the area, fortunately, even working as an Eaton representative for a power plant.

People at Georgia Power saw his resume and knew they wanted him with them. They called and asked how he'd like coming to work there.

It was another easy transition to that team. At Georgia Power, Tolbert is pretty much doing exactly what he was doing while working for Eaton, projects for electrical switch gear. He works on projects for the equipment in the low voltage switchyard as well as the high voltage switchyard.

Military Spouse, a Completely Different Trajectory

After basic training and advanced individual training, Stephanie Roper returned to Austin to attend Texas A&M. She soon began thinking though about transitioning to full-time service as an officer candidate and making a career out of the military.

But she had served in the nineteen-nineties. Post-Desert Storm, the government began downsizing the military. Army installations were closing all over the country. She was feeling very uneasy about this. She shifted gears and married Rick Roper, thus becoming a military spouse. This was a completely different trajectory and quite a complicated path going forward.

While they were both native Texans, Stephanie Roper and her husband had taken very separate paths in the Army. She had been a non-commissioned officer. He was a West Point graduate, a former Army football quarterback and an infantry officer.

When the Army started disbanding many military units and installations, a number of their friends were dual military. In the military, personnel who are both in the military can request joint domicile, meaning both are stationed at the same duty location at the same time. However, there's no guarantee that both will be stationed at the same duty location. In fact, about ninety percent of Roper's peers didn't live together like most married couples.

Roper and her husband decided to make his career primary and her career secondary. For a dozen years, she followed his career all over the country and was the consummate military spouse. He had a very successful career with multiple combat tours and retired as a lieutenant colonel. But they moved around quite a lot.

In the officer corps, you get moved to your next job and your next duty location when the military wants to move you. And you move anywhere they choose. You might be somewhere for six months or two years.

In Roper's case, they never lived anywhere more than two years. In fact, they lived in some of their duty stations for no more than six months. In most instances, by the time Roper settled into her new home and began seeking employment, which she found very difficult to get hired as a military spouse, it was time to pack up and move to the next duty station. Many companies didn't want to invest the time or money in her, since they knew she might be leaving rather soon.

Roper spent the remainder of her time in the Army Reserves moving around the country supporting her husband, an active-duty soldier. Austin Peay State University, based in Clarksville, Tennessee, granted her a bachelor's degree in health and physical education in 2001 and a master's degree in health and human performance in 2002 while she and her husband moved from one duty station to another.

She also had a litany of jobs working for the U.S. Military Academy, American Red Cross, multiple departments of health and human services across New York State, and as a teacher and high school track and cross-country coach. She wasn't a subject matter expert in any one thing. Rather, she honed a variety of skillsets during this time.

In 2004, the Ropers landed at West Point, the U.S. Military Academy. However, soon thereafter, because her husband was an infantry officer, he was deployed to the Middle East.

Typically, during most deployments, a military spouse might pack up and move home. But Roper had started to make a career for herself at West Point, as a civilian employee. She worked for the department of physical education and then conducted research for the Army's physical fitness program.

While her husband was deployed, she began preparing herself for the next phase of their journey, his retirement from the Army and her own desire for a more substantial career. A few months into his deployment, she found a job posting for Consolidated Edison, a company she knew nothing about, located in a city she had only visited a dozen or so times, New York. The posting was for a job as a specialist in a group called talent management, a section of the human resources department, running their leadership and career development programs for incoming college graduates, and employees transitioning from union roles to management roles.

She applied for the job and instantly connected with her interviewer. During that first session, the interviewer acknowledged Roper's military service and asked her questions about what it was like to serve in the military. The interviewer even divulged to Roper that both she and her husband were initially hired by Con Edison in the post-Vietnam War period to work on building testing skills and aptitude for the war's veterans that the utility wanted to bring into its workforce.

This personal connection bloomed into a job offer. And so, in January of 2007, Roper began working in Con Edison's human resources department, and did that through December of 2014, eight years later.

Around the six-year mark, she even served as manager of recruitment, working specifically on attracting veterans, minorities, women from non-traditional career paths, and individuals with disabilities. She also worked on the Governor's Troops to Energy Jobs Initiative and was an advocate for the industry's Center for Energy Workforce Development.

This discovery of her niche in the workplace was momentous. She finally found what felt like the perfect fit. In this role, she was able to recognize the contributions and skill sets that not just veterans, but veteran's spouses and children could bring to the table. It was not only rewarding, but also a great effort on behalf of the company.

Her transition into the company had been relatively easy. It was the geographic change that was the hardest part. As a native Texan, Roper felt that adjusting to New York's culture was the most challenging.

In the military, she had lived in seven states over twelve years. Yet New York was her first duty station in a northern state. It was tough getting accustomed to the weather. She had never had to dress in layers before.

Those who took her in at Con Edison helped her move past her comfort zone and learn some street smarts. Coming from her background living on military installations, even things like locking her doors and minding her purse were foreign to her. Roper learned to embrace it. She had so many first-time experiences that she could easily write her own book on everything that happened to her in the first year of working in the big city.

Roper's corporate transition had more to do with learning how to acclimate and assimilate into the culture, which was its own scheme to figure out. She quickly learned that the corporate sector was much more competitive in nature, and not as family oriented as the military. But she applied her experiences of moving frequently – which required resiliency, flexibility, and strong interpersonal skills – to help with the transition.

There were some areas that required additional time to fully understand. For one, you don't have to sell yourself in the military. Your reputation, work ethic, and military record are pivotal to your success. Promotions are simply a next step. There is no need to be cutthroat or laser-focused on getting ahead of others if you work hard, are successful at team building, and execute. You are rewarded by being promoted to the next level at the next milestone.

Your work product and your leadership skills are what lands you the next job. There is no jockeying for positions. In the utilities industry, we promote change, growth, and variety. How well you interview is a big part of landing a new job.

Prior to joining Con Edison, Roper had not had a job for more than two years for a while. This was actually attractive to the company after hearing why she had so many positions across so many different areas. She was a constant learner, who they knew would be a great asset to the company, and who was eager to build her own career.

In fact, a stable job where she could build a career was what was so desirable to Roper. She hadn't had that level of stability since she was moving from place to place to place following her husband's career.

However, old habits die hard. Instead of moving physically, Roper has moved through various roles throughout her now fifteen years with Con Edison, changing positions every couple of years through department changes or promotions. The ability to continue to constantly learn has been a surprising combination of both comfort and motivation to get to the next level.

Roper is one of three co-leads serving on the executive board for the Veterans of Con Edison. It's an employee resource group that she along with a few of her peers put together four years ago. Its mission is to cultivate comradery of veterans within the company by advocating and being a voice for veterans, providing support and networking opportunities such as mentoring, community outreach, career development, and cultural awareness activities.

The most difficult part for many transitioning from the military, is that in the service, your personal life is not just your personal life. Your personal life and your military life are co-mingled. In many cases, you live in the same neighborhood as your boss and your peers. Children go to school together and are friends. If you or a member of your family gets in trouble in their personal life, the chain of command knows about it almost immediately.

Working in the civilian sector is, of course, different. And the transition can be difficult for both the service member and their dependents. Finding that same sense of family out of the gate is what the Veterans of Con Edison employee resource group is about. The goal is to mentor, guide, and help former service members with their transition so that they're successful. And so that the company is successful in retaining some of the strongest leaders who know what it's like to sacrifice.

In her current role, Roper serves as the general manager for supply chain – stores operations. The promotion to this job had come as something of a surprise. She had been section manager for Bronx/Westchester electric construction networks, for environmental operations.

It was an honor to be selected for the role of general manager in the fall of 2019. It was also overwhelming. She found herself now working in supply chain, which she knew nothing about. Although just a short time ago, she hadn't known anything about electric operations either. But in both positions, she excelled and progressed rather quickly.

These days, her team of over two hundred employees supplies every single item used at Con Edison and Orange & Rockland (except for the vehicles). Roper is responsible for working with her peers to source, procure, store, transport, and distribute every pipe, wire, and transformer that goes on the system.

During the pandemic, she also worked on procuring, storing, and distributing every mask, Lysol wipe, hand sanitizer, etc. for the entire company. With the significant supply chain disruptions across the world, her job has become even more complex. But she has learned far more than she would have, had the pandemic not taken place, because of the accelerated pace.

Pictured: Bill Krieger (top left), Monique Carter (top right, front row far left), storm restoration efforts following a tornado near Onalaska, Texas (center, photo courtesy of Chad Simon), Kelcey Brown (bottom, leftmost in group of three)

Pictured: DeAnne Ostrowski (top left, far right), Chad Craven (top right), Kelcey Brown (center, right), Zach Johnson, Sam Houston Electric Cooperative line technician, uses climbing hooks to climb a pole near Seven Oaks, Texas (bottom left, photo courtesy of Chad Simon), Sam Houston Electric Cooperative line technicians prepare a pole on the ground following a tornado near Moscow, Texas (bottom right, photo courtesy of Chad Simon)

Pictured: Rob Douglass (top left), Scott Bolton (top right), storm restoration efforts following a tornado near Onalaska, Texas (center, photo courtesy of Chad Simon), Kersha Brown (bottom)

CHAPTER FOUR

Veterans in the Utilities Industry

Qualities, Qualifications, Differences

Some of them climb the poles, clothed in their protective gear. Some at headquarters are climbing the corporate ladder, instead in their suits. They're all over America's utilities, in logistics, operations, human resources, engineering, accounting; everywhere really. Often the tip of the spear after storms, many man the crews that go up the poles as soon as the wind dies down to thirty-five miles per hour.

They had been Soldiers, or Sailors, or Marines, or Airmen, or Coast Guardsmen. For some, it's been a decade or two since they wore the uniform of the United States Army, Navy, Marine Corps, Air Force, or Coast Guard. For others, they're just now settling in, getting acclimated to the civilian workforce, their discharge papers still feeling fresh.

The veterans in the utilities industry are distinct from each other as any cross section of the country's citizenry. They may have grown up in Nevada, Nebraska, or New Jersey, in Minnesota or Mississippi, or from any star on the flag. Women and men, of every color and background, their accents and appearance are individual. In our industry, though, their similarities are striking.

The veterans among us in the utilities industry have qualities that are as easy to recognize as they are uniquely fitted to utility service. Yes, sir. Yes, ma'am. Their politeness and respect for authority stands out. Their dedication to mission and safety does too. It can seem to be almost an obsession, to those of us who haven't been a military service member, whenever small talk instantly gives way to the job at hand.

These qualities, of such great value in the work of utilities, can at the same time be barriers in the workplace between veterans and those who have never worn the uniform. When it's break time, to cite one example, and the daily routine is stop by a Starbucks, there can be an awkwardness about putting aside a task incomplete, even temporarily. When there's a protocol that's always been bypassed, there can be a stilted conversation about going by the book.

Then there's the dicey divergences on what constitutes leadership. Most of the utility workforce that aren't veterans can have an awfully hard time appreciating that the veterans they work with received extensive leadership training and experience notwithstanding their young age or years in our industry. A twenty-eight-year-old may have led a company in combat or commanded a billion-dollar asset on the open seas or in the intercontinental skies. It can be humbling for them, and frustrating at times, to see that training and experience count for so little with their new bosses and peers at a utility.

And then there's the comradery of military service and the lack thereof at the utility job site or office where everyone drops everything and rushes home at the end of the workday for dinner with the family, or to catch the kid's soccer game. It can be disconcerting to say the least when the memories of a close-knit company living together twenty-four-seven, particularly when deployed far from home, are remembered.

How are the utilities industry's veterans doing? What makes their contributions to the provision of electric, natural gas, and water utility service so compelling? What challenges are they facing and facing down in their civilian careers?

Their Jobs Run the Gamut

In utilities, there are veterans in every facet of the business. They're in HR, IT, T&D, DSM, Comms, Ops, you name it. They're wearing hard hats and protective glasses at the plant or a blazer over a button-down or blouse at the corporate office.

They came straight from the branch they served in without a hitch. Or they first found themselves going down a blind alley or two before finding that utility service is a fine fit when all you've really known is military service.

For many of them, fitting in our industry was a rather seamless journey. Though for some, they're still on their journey. And seamless isn't how they'd describe it, at least when downloading with buddies from their last deployment.

You might know a vet at the job, or maybe more than one. Yet you might not know them very well. One may sit at a desk a couple of cubicles over from you at work. Another may eat a salad a couple of tables away at the company cafeteria. Perhaps you've exchanged pleasantries and participated in the same March Madness pool. But that's about it.

So, let's really visit with a few, and flesh out their experiences within our industry. First off, let's visit with Bill Krieger.

Nobody Shot at Him

Krieger served in both the U.S. Army and Navy. That's right, both. We didn't ask whether he sides with the Black Knights or Midshipmen in the Army-Navy Game.

Now he's at the investor-owned utility, Consumers Energy, which provides electric and natural gas utility service to communities throughout Michigan.

Krieger had been the manager for electric operations in the Flint/Tri-Cities region of Flint, Saginaw, Midland, and Bay City in central Michigan. Though he was recently made the veterans affairs program manager for the company. Which is indicative of how Consumers Energy is prioritizing the recruiting, retaining, and supporting of veterans.

It was way back in 1994 when Krieger left the Navy. He then bounced around at a couple of different jobs. His transition from the military to the civilian workforce wasn't at all smooth. Jarring is a better way to describe it. Why? It was a combination of things.

Krieger struggled. He was used to having a task and purpose and having set goals as is characteristic within the military. And he was used to understanding the overall mission, and other critical tidbits, like what it takes to get promoted.

In the civilian jobs that Krieger held in this early period of his transition, he just did not feel the purpose as in military service. He didn't feel like he was doing anything that was going to make a difference or that mattered much.

Krieger also attributes some of the struggle to his perception, often borne out by his experiences, that many civilian employers do not understand the military mindset. For instance, a veteran doesn't necessarily need to be told by his supervisor specifically how to accomplish a goal. The vet does need to know what the goal is.

In the military, this is called the commander's intent. When Krieger was a company commander, his battalion commander would give him the intent. Krieger would then be responsible for executing it.

Part of the reason employers hire former military is because veterans are generally self-starters. They get stuff done. But in the civilian world, there's commonly a lack of that commander's intent or the equivalent. So, he felt, that it's uncertain what your employer exactly wants you to accomplish on a given day.

Krieger eventually landed a job later in 1994 as an electric lines dispatcher at Consumers Energy. And then he discovered to his delight that the culture at the company was strikingly close to his military experience. There was a clear chain of command. And the work in operations was, to Krieger, exciting. He also found a similar camaraderie at the company, as he had experienced in the Navy. Krieger could see where he fit in.

Initially, in his new career, he concentrated on operations. If a team wasn't doing its job correctly, not strictly following protocols, the consequences could be deathly. But if they diligently train and perform with consistency, day-in and day-out, this removes some of that danger and uncertainty.

Electric and natural gas utility services make a positive impact on the lives of others. At Consumers Energy, there was finally a sense of purpose behind everything he was doing.

The company promoted Krieger after two years to gas and electric service designer and then after another two years to senior technical analyst. While in that new position, managing software development and implementation for the company, he additionally resumed military service, though with the Army rather than Navy.

For the Army, he served as first line supervisor at various locations worldwide for the next three and a half years through the 9/11 period, until September of 2003. And subsequently as operations manager for two years into late 2005 and operations director for four and a half years into 2010.

At some times stateside with Consumers Energy, where he was promoted again and again, to gas operations planning and scheduling lead and then to gas and electric design team leader, and at other times with the Army throughout the world, Krieger somehow managed to assume increasing responsibility in both the civilian and military environments. But it was hardly easy on him.

In October of 2007, Krieger stepped off the battlefield in Iraq, as an Army operations director, and onto an airplane that brought him home. Just two weeks later, he was driving his car to the office in Lansing, Michigan, resuming his job at Consumers Energy as gas and electric design team leader.

When he got to his office, he thought to himself, man, this is going to be a fantastic day. But this wasn't because he had a great job. And it wasn't because the sun was shining that morning. It was instead because nobody had shot at him. And it was because nothing blew up. His next thought was, holy crap, I'm crazy. Nobody thinks like this.

Plus, it was proving to be very difficult for Krieger to be compassionate when people came to him with their problems. It was another lesson for him to learn, to acknowledge that other people's struggles are real to them. It would not work for him to say, oh well, I just got back from combat. Your struggle is stupid. But, Krieger admits, he did think that way a couple of times.

Krieger says that at Consumers Energy, there's a lot of respect for the military. Management values the lessons that veteran employees learned while in military service and what they bring to the table in leadership.

Of course, he adds, the military is just a cross-section of society. Not everybody has every skill that you hear about former military. But Consumers Energy has been good about utilizing the skills that a vet does have. And the company has also been good about understanding the military mindset.

Krieger took us through how he struggled when he came back from combat. It was very hard for him to get back onto the right path. He later started having a lot of problems with anxiety. He didn't tell anyone at first.

But one day, he found himself on his way to work thinking that if he didn't change something soon, he was going to jump off a building. So, he called his supervisor, talked to human resources, and later went on sick leave for a little while to get his head straight. In the meantime, he and others realized that he needed to step back from leadership for a while. Because the struggle was causing him a lot of problems.

At the age of fifty-five, it would have been quite natural for the company to reflexively encourage him to retire. But Consumers Energy didn't. Instead, management said, we value you, and you still have a lot to give. How about if we put you in this position to work with other veterans? Krieger says that response was characteristic of how they treat veterans there.

Military people do indeed have a deeper understanding of military people. No question about it. Because among former military there's a great deal of comradery and a sense of family.

There is a somewhat similar atmosphere at his company, as Krieger sees it. Yet, he feels the bond between people is different. Former military really do understand the same inside jokes, the same language, and even how each other is feeling. The shared experience of military service is something, Krieger believes, you simply cannot synthesize. That's the beauty of utilities maintaining employee resource groups, or ERGs, like the veterans advisory panel at Consumers Energy that Krieger is a founding member and past co-chair of.

Out in the Field with the Linemen

Now let's look at the experiences within our industry of a former Marine. Chad Simon retired from the U.S. Marine Corps in 2014, after nearly sixteen years of service, primarily as a combat photographer/chief. Simon had supervised teams at Marine Corps Air Station New River in Jacksonville, North Carolina, in Okinawa, Japan, and in Iraq.

After leaving the Marines, he went back to Kansas, where he was born and raised. And to Fort Hays State University to finish his degree, where he had started his college studies a long time before, in 1996, eighteen years earlier. He and his family moved to Hays, Kansas and they enrolled the kids in school.

After two and a half years, Simon finished his bachelor's degree. The degree wasn't in journalism, which was what he concentrated on in the Marines, but in communications. After all that work as a journalist, being a reporter no longer appealed to him. Public relations now interested him more.

One time, during his last summer in Hays, in 2016, he saw an advertisement for a communications intern at Midwest Energy, an electric and natural gas cooperative serving forty counties in central and western Kansas. He applied for the internship and started that summer. His communications manager there was a former Navy officer, though he had originally enlisted, and he had also worked as a Navy journalist.

Simon loved working at Midwest Energy that summer. Many aspects of being in the military transferred seamlessly to working at a co-op. Being part of something that is bigger than any one individual, and providing a service to communities, felt very comfortable.

At the internship, he had begun to introduce himself to fellow employees as a thirty-eight-year-old intern. One asked, he recalls, if he enjoyed working there. When Simon said he was really enjoying it, they told him that if he wanted to stay in the cooperative industry, he should check out the Touchstone Energy Cooperative's website.

Simon had amassed some decent experience during his short internship. He even documented a restoration of utility service after a storm, including the high winds, utilizing both his topography and photography backgrounds. Then, as he was finishing up the internship, he began to look through job postings.

He applied to co-ops across the Southeast for jobs in communications. He and his family were looking to move back to North Carolina, or to Tennessee, Florida, South Carolina, or Virginia. While Texas wasn't their top choice, they also looked there since they had family and some friends in the Lone Star State. Simon eventually secured some interviews. But he still lacked sufficient experience at civilian workplaces.

When he finally finished his degree in 2016, Simon started at Fort Riley, Kansas, working for the Army's first infantry division as a civilian contractor in their public affairs office. He was there for two years, and at the same time kept applying for co-op jobs and kept an eye on the Touchstone interview page as well. He applied for a lot of jobs. And was trying to figure out how to support his family of six including a child with an intellectual disability.

Simon found that he liked the service industry and was even applying to work for charities. In the meantime, he and his wife were driving forces in starting northwest Kansas' Down Syndrome Society in support of their daughter. They raised over two thousand dollars for Down Syndrome research by running in the 2013 Marine Corps Marathon that traditionally finishes up at the Iwo Jima Memorial in Arlington, Virginia. They went on to raise more money at the 2015 Chicago Marathon.

Later, they continued this endeavor in the New York City and San Francisco Marathons. The society they helped start continues to host a charity golf tournament annually, benefitting over eighteen counties in northwest Kansas. And it helped fund an inclusive playground in Hays.

Simon applied for two promising jobs in mid-2018, positions that were open at Surry Yadkin Electric in Dobson, North Carolina and Sam Houston Electric Cooperative in Livingston, Texas. It was his last effort at job applications. Applying for anything later would have forced him to move his family during the school year.

He interviewed with Surry Yadkin Electric and loved it. Yet, a little over a week later he interviewed with Sam Houston Electric. The fit there was what they were looking for, exactly, a photographer with writing experience. So, the Simon family packed up, left Kansas, and came down to Texas.

Sam Houston Electric, a rural electric cooperative, provides more than fifty thousand members/customers with electric utility service in a southeast region of the Lone Star State. The counties it serves are to the northeast of Houston.

As a communications specialist at Sam Houston Electric, Simon loves getting out into the field with the cooperative's linemen and especially being in their environments during storm restorations. He really likes to show off what they do, and what they go through to keep the lights on. At the co-op, to Simon, it's all about providing an essential service to the community, above worrying about the utility's bottom line.

Didn't Know His Political Party

Thus far, we've visited with Bill Krieger, who ended up in our industry in the upper Midwest. And Chad Simon, who ended up at a cooperative in Texas. Now we turn to a vet working at a utility in the Pacific Northwest.

It was 1993, an important turning point for Scott Bolton. After his four years in the U.S. Army, as a signals intelligence analyst, Bolton returned to the Pacific Northwest and to his education a changed man. He was, admittedly, before serving in the military, unmotivated and unwilling to apply himself in high school. Now, he was a highly disciplined student. Making use of the G.I. Bill, he received his degree three years later, a bachelor's in political science from Portland State University.

Also in 1993, as he was getting started at Portland State, he simultaneously began a work study job. At the time, the approved work study sites of the local Veterans Administration were either the medical center or the regional office. Then, as fate would have it, Congressman Ron Wyden made available a work study position.

Bolton managed to hear about this opportunity. After hitting it off with the district director, the young veteran landed a spot in a congressional office. He recalls, he didn't even know Wyden's political party before the morning of the interview. Though Wyden, a member of the Democratic Party, had already served in the U.S. House of Representatives for a dozen years.

Three years later, when Wyden ran for the U.S. Senate, Bolton became a part of the freshman Senator's permanent staff. A work study position had now turned into a full-time job, coincidentally about the time that Bolton graduated Portland State.

His first job with the congressional office was to move to Bend. It's far inland, in the center of the state of Oregon, and one hundred sixty miles southeast of Portland. There Bolton opened a new congressional outreach office.

The goal was to provide more constituent access to Wyden's efforts. Until Wyden had won the Senate seat, constituent offices were typically located within the state's cities along the Pacific coast, in Portland and Salem.

Oregon's was (and still is) a culturally divided state, with areas that are predominately urban or rural, and liberal or conservative. Senator Wyden was determined to do better in rural areas. It was Bolton's job to help make that happen. Thinking back about this experience, Bolton feels that his time in the military, working with diverse groups of people, allowed him to easily adapt to the local culture of central Oregon. Actually, it was a rather comfortable transition for him.

After working for Congressman Wyden for three years and for Senator Wyden for a couple more, and earning a master's degree in business administration, Bolton joined PacifiCorp in 2004. He started out as manager for government affairs. Before long he was promoted to director for government affairs and then to vice president for government affairs.

Two years after Bolton joined PacifiCorp, the Portland-based investor-owned electric utility was purchased by Berkshire Hathaway Energy. PacifiCorp now provides electric utility service to nearly two million customers in Oregon, California, Washington, Utah, Wyoming, and Idaho. And Bolton is currently the company's senior vice president for transmission development.

Having worked in government for a while, for Congressman and Senator Wyden, Bolton had been quite keen to build a career in the private sector. But the mission of public service remained close to his heart. It was another natural transition, going to work for a utility serving the public interest, and working there in government affairs, embodying the best of both worlds.

Bolton believes that the military is presently doing a better job providing services for transitioning veterans. When he left military life, he showed up at the Presidio (then still a military base in San Francisco) after a fourteen-hour flight, spent two to three hours signing papers, and was handed a bus ticket. It was, from the Army, so long, and have a nice life.

These days, the Army and the other military services seem to be doing a better job leveraging resumes, skill building tools, and job searching sites to help veterans walk along a smoother path to the civilian world. And benefits for families and continuing education seem to be expanding. Now it's as though most veterans come out expecting to step directly into the job market.

His company's leadership has come to recognize, through their collaboration with the Edison Electric Institute and other peer groups, that there are a significant number of veteran employees across the utilities industry. And that there's a positive military-affiliated subculture within many of the companies.

It has now become a real priority at PacifiCorp to keep demonstrating that the company is veteran friendly. A parallel priority is to foster an environment of mutual understanding and respect between veteran and non-veteran employees to create an even stronger corporate culture.

Trying to be a Swiss Army Knife

There are many veterans within utilities that are based in the Southeast. One such vet is Chad Craven, a computer network administrator for Pee Dee Electric Cooperative.

Pee Dee's headquarters is in Wadesboro, North Carolina. It provides electric utility service to more than twenty thousand members/consumers in the south-central part of the state, east of Charlotte, including parts of Richmond and Anson counties.

When Craven made the decision to retire from the U.S. Marine Corps after twenty-four years, he received a call during his retirement ceremony from someone who went to school with his wife. The caller had heard Craven was moving back to the Carolinas and said there was a job he might be interested in. Before long, Craven was in a phone interview for the position he continues to work in now.

Craven quickly realized, even during the in-person interview, and then after he was hired, that the sense of community and brotherhood in the utilities industry is very much like what he had experienced in the Marines. He hasn't had a bad day at work in his five years working with Pee Dee.

When he first came to the company, there was a whole lot for him to learn. First, there was the lingo. Of course, he had researched Pee Dee before doing his interview. But Craven still knew next to nothing, or nothing at all, about large transmission equipment, electrical circuits, the phases of power substations, and the like.

With no frame of reference whatsoever, he was fortunate that everyone he encountered took him in and showed him what to do. He aimed to be a sort of Swiss army knife within the organization. Now that's a role he believes veterans lend themselves easily to.

A veteran is used to contributing to the team in unusual and a range of capacities. If the trash needs to be taken out, if a light bulb needs to be changed, if something needs to be unloaded off a truck, someone is there. People are just used to doing that in the military. That doesn't go away when they transition into the civilian workforce.

In a typical day, Craven can go from fixing information technology problems to talking to someone about a relationship. It makes him feel good that people seek his advice, and that this is a skill he brings with him to any role he assumes.

Craven went from managing nearly five hundred Marines and millions of dollars' worth of equipment to working on anything he can get his hands on at the company. He spends his time avoiding idleness by learning about any and all aspects of his company and its equipment.

If he volunteers to work at a community festival or another kind of outreach event, he wants to be able to respond intelligently even if someone asks him questions about something unrelated to his specific job. Craven and others there at Pee Dee have branched out into research on subjects like electric vehicles.

It all goes back to working on becoming the Swiss army knife that his company needs, being well-rounded to benefit members throughout the co-op organization. He says that this mentality also originates from his time in the military. There, you're encouraged to diversify and cultivate this well-roundedness.

Anytime there are major storms, Craven is right there to support the linemen. Obviously, he's not out doing active line work. Though he doesn't have a problem throwing on rain gear and helping flag to keep traffic moving, or cranking up a chainsaw, or doing whatever it is that needs to be done.

None of that has anything to do with being a computer network administrator. But, for Craven, it keeps things fresh. When you finally take the uniform off for the last time, he believes, you just have to keep things fresh.

Moving Up in the Big Apple

Another vet who told us her story was DeAnne Ostrowski, who is presently a general manager for electric operations at Consolidated Edison, based in New York City. But when Ostrowski first left the U.S. Navy, she started out working for a health and nutrition company.

Later, she went with Bradley-Morris, a military recruiting firm. At the time, the firm was placing former officers in engineering or logistics jobs. When Ostrowski went for a job placement, they had a job opening in sales. At first, she wasn't interested. But they explained that she would be "selling" a military veteran candidate. She would be explaining to companies what these applicants had to offer.

Bradley-Morris turned out to be a very good transition. She worked on the account side and was able to see trends in the industry. Ostrowski was also able to talk to candidates who went into different companies and then soon left. She learned why they wanted a change. In the back of her mind, she was building a list of all these different things she was looking for in a company, for her next career move.

Then, when she wasn't even looking to leave Bradley-Morris yet, Con Edison came looking to hire candidates. To her, it was the perfect fit. And it has been over the sixteen years at the company.

Her transition went very smoothly. Ostrowski started out as a supervisor in Con Edison's installation and apparatus group in the Bronx. After working there for about two years, she moved up to a planner level position as a field technical specialist working in the overhead lines area. She dealt with all the lines above and responding to disruptive storm systems that would come through.

Next, she worked as a section manager, handling a diverse group in electric operations. After that, Ostrowski got a promotion to be a general manager in stores operations. She had the leadership skills they were looking for. So, she went into Con Edison's stores operations, covering major warehouses in the service territory of Orange and Rockland Utilities, north of New York City, in Astoria, Queens, and at sixteen satellite locations.

She was later asked to transition to environmental health and safety. Ostrowski was concerned that she didn't have the environmental expertise to succeed in her position. But it ended up working out well.

She was then brought back to electric operations to serve as a general manager there. More recently, she has moved to working with the emergency preparedness group.

Vet CEO

Kelcey Brown was always sure that her military career in the U.S. Navy would last the time of her five-year commitment and not any longer. She had served mostly as a photographer on the huge aircraft carrier USS Nimitz.

Brown then enrolled at the University of Wyoming immediately after her service ended. She describes it as starting her life. Even though she had been offered opportunities to go into a combat camera group and to tour in Europe with an admiral, as his photographer, she turned that down in favor of getting to school. She was laser-focused on finishing both her bachelor's and master's degrees in four years.

Brown says that she has always been a numbers person. Math comes to her easily. This might explain why she got her college degree in regulatory economics.

Brown's program at U. of Wyoming focused on regulation. Economics is a beautiful fit for regulation, in her thinking, because it's pure theory. The goal is to stimulate perfect competition, something that she finds fascinating.

She had the opportunity to apply this fascination first at an internship with the Illinois Commerce Commission. When she later graduated in 2003, many utilities were not hiring due to the aftermath of the recent energy crisis. So, she ended up working at Blackfoot Telecommunications in Missoula, Montana, and stayed there for almost four years.

She then learned about her true interest, electric utilities, during her next four years at the Oregon Public Utility Commission. Her position there was as a senior economist.

In 2011, she was hired by Portland, Oregon-based PacifiCorp, a subsidiary of Berkshire Hathaway Energy, and eventually worked her way up into operations and energy supply management. From 2011 to 2020, Brown served in various regulatory, commercial, and operational roles, most recently as the vice president of energy supply management. In this position she was responsible for the energy imbalance market analytics, policy research, contract administration, and short-term load forecasting.

Then, in late 2020, she was offered a special opportunity. She was to manage MidAmerican Energy as its president and CEO, a role she assumed in January of 2021.

Brown attributes much of her ambition to her passion for learning. She also credits Berkshire Hathaway Energy's leadership development program. Of course, she does feel some luck played a role as well. But she certainly put herself in a good position to encounter these fortuitous opportunities.

She remembers always taking on as much work as possible. This is not because she simply wanted more work to do. But because the subject matter truly interested her. She was constantly working to fill in any gaps in her knowledge about her company and the industry.

Front Lines to Power Lineman

Desert Storm was over. The country was now downsizing the military. While home from the war zone, Jeff Benson considered reenlisting in the U.S. Marine Corps. But, by then, he had something of an attitude change in him. He was ready to move on to the next challenge.

The last decision left was whether he wanted to be an electrician or a power lineman. How did Benson turn so readily to the utilities?

When he was growing up, in southern Minnesota, the next-door neighbors began a family business of electricians. He would go and help them as a kid. Benson would fetch wire nuts off the van and the like, as they were working in a house.

Meanwhile, across the alleyway from where he grew up, was another neighbor who was a lineman for what is now Xcel Energy. This neighbor had a bucket truck that was always home.

Yet another neighbor, a couple houses north, was the operations manager for the City of St. James. There he was, surrounded by these strong men, who were also veterans, in their case of the second world war and the Korean war. When making his decision, Benson was reminded of that bucket truck. He thought it might be cool to go up into the air again, albeit with a very different setting and stakes from his time in the Marines.

He formulated a plan to go to a vocational-technical school to become a power lineman. The transition, however, wasn't a smooth one.

Even though Benson was back home, he wasn't the same person who had left. That made getting together with old friends difficult. It took him a little while to adjust. When Benson was asked about what made this difficult, he couldn't quite place the feeling. Surely, many other veterans empathize with this strange adjustment period.

Initially, after Benson left the military, he was living with some single school friends. They had full-time jobs as factory supervisors. Benson was working part-time and still going to school.

They would go to breakfast on Sunday mornings. He recalls that his friends would wake him up on those mornings by poking his foot with a broom handle, from a safe distance. His time in the Marines had left its mark. Benson would often awaken with the instinct to defend himself. He says that this constant alertness has lessened overtime. But it has never gone away.

This feeling of vulnerability extends to other facets of his life as well. For example, when he travels by airline, he cannot bring a weapon as a concealed carry holder. So, he might travel with a small pocketknife in his checked luggage. This way, when he gets to his destination, he can feel a little safer.

Benson can't carry a weapon at work either. But he might carry a skinning knife for wires. He explains that all of this is a state of mind, self-preservation, the need to feel ready to protect yourself.

Benson went to the lineman's school program in Jackson, Minnesota, at a vocational-technical college. It was a one-year program at the time. But the problem was, it was initially full when he meant to start.

In the meantime, he worked at a local factory, until his veteran service officer called. The man explained to Benson that he couldn't get him into that program he wanted just yet. Though the department head would meet with him. And he might be able to finish some general education classes prior to starting. Benson agreed.

To his surprise, the department head was a Marine in the Vietnam War. The two of them immediately hit it off. Benson was enrolled. He did his general education work and finally got into the lineman's program the following year. And he could now go to school for half-days, focusing on the program since he had finished his general coursework.

Now, with some free time, he called South Central Electric Association to see if they needed summer help during the construction season. They did.

South Central Electric Association is based in St. James, Minnesota. The rural electric cooperative in the southern part of the state serves forty-seven hundred members/customers.

Benson was hired part-time, working with South Central Electric for two years while he completed his schooling. Then, a few months before he was meant to graduate, the foreman decided to retire at the year's end. The operations manager asked Benson if he was interested in a full-time job.

Over the years, Benson has risen from apprentice lineman to journeyman and then applied for an opening to become foreman of a crew. Later, he was selected to serve in his current role as line superintendent.

When considering the value of hiring veterans, Benson notes that veterans are used to dealing with obstacles, even those as simple as inclement weather. Veterans are taught to be flexible, to adapt to new problems as they arise, and collaborate to develop a new plan.

Working in utilities can be similar in this way. As a storm rolls through, it's the linemen who are coming in afterwards to restore power. Not only are there long physical hours, but there's a necessary level of competence to maintain.

He also believes there is a lot of pride to be had in doing this work. You can help people, keep the lights on. And at the end of his day, you can go home, take a shower, and sleep in your own bed.

Renewable Engineer

Sean Grier left the U.S. Army, the Army's Corp of Engineers specifically, after eight years of service, in March of 1997. Grier then went straight back to school, to George Mason University. There, he earned two undergraduate degrees by 2001, in electrical engineering and actuarial mathematics.

Shortly after graduation, in January of 2002, he joined what is now Duke Energy. The company was still called Cinergy back in those days, where he started working, and based in the Cincinnati area.

It was different for him dealing with the civilian sector. But he adapted. Within months, he started traveling to construction sites, acting more like a project engineer over the following years.

Cinergy and Charlotte, North Carolina-based Duke merged in 2006. Grier's group, Duke Energy's generation services, was a non-regulated organization starting to go into renewable energy. Four years later, Grier continued his studies, for a master's in electrical engineering at Gonzaga University, while still a principal engineer at Duke. He completed his master's in 2014 and before long was promoted by the company to manager.

Grier now serves as a director of the renewables engineering division for Duke Energy's sustainable solutions function. He's leading a team of electrical and mechanical engineers to perform engineering activities all over the country at the company's wind, solar, and battery storage sites.

He feels that he has always applied his military principles in his civilian job. The leadership skills and mission orientation he gained from the Army consistently and positively affect his work.

Air

Coming out of the military, Quintin Gaddis says it was really by accident that he went into the utilities industry. He had always worked with electronics throughout his career in the U.S. Air Force, for the C-141 Starlifter and C-5 Galaxy cargo planes. His power industry experience started not in the industry per se but with an Air Products & Chemical facility in Middletown, Ohio.

Gaddis was intrigued by his work operating the power station at this air separation plant. It was while working to build a substation there that he became interested in moving to an electric utility.

He realized that the whole concept of the air separation profession was closely associated to how an aircraft engine operated. So, whenever he started learning how to run the plant and more about the substation piece, it just kept going back to his aviation experience. He recognized that the power industry operated around machines that were essentially aircraft engines. When he thought about an electric power plant, he simply thought about an aircraft engine turned upside down.

After working all over the place with Air Products & Chemicals, he was encouraged to seek opportunities at the nearby utility, Dayton Power & Light.

An individual at that company helped him bring together all the elements of his career. He could now combine his experiences from the military and Air Products & Chemical. Gaddis later completed his industry certification to become a system operator.

His experience as an airman continues to influence his actions in the workplace in the utilities industry. The structure, policy, and procedure behind everything that he does is all habit from the Air Force. Those Air Force experiences are the foundation for everything he is doing now.

For instance, everything he does starts with safety and good training. It's his group's job to ensure that all of their work starts with having safe and efficient power transformation from power plant to customer. He is also responsible for leading the group that maintains the protection equipment in substations. Any time a car hits a pole, or a tree falls on a line, he works to protect substation operations and ensure no further damage within the infrastructure. Also, any time there is an outage, the protection schemes that his group implements isolate the outage to a small section in order to prevent large quantities of people from being out of power.

Gaddis thinks his present work as senior manager of substation and meter operations for Portland General Electric is absolutely amazing. It changes every day. So, it really excites him. He works in the power plants, the power stations, and with the apparatus out on the distribution lines. He also gets to work with everybody from their system operating group.

As a former system operator, he says it's great to communicate with them and line operations. More importantly, to Gaddis, the people are truly what makes his job very special.

He explains that the most rewarding thing about working at Portland General is supporting the great people that work there. It's an exciting career, an exciting opportunity, and he's had some wonderful experiences. Just to be able to watch, whether it's a new apprentice learning a craft, or seeing how crews get the lights back on and restored to smiling customers.

Intelligence

Before it was time to graduate and receive his bachelor's in infrastructure assurance from the University of Texas at San Antonio, U.S. Army veteran Brandon Pixley visited the career counseling office once again and entered his name into an internship database. Less than a month later, he received a call from a recruiter asking if he would be interested in applying for a paid summer internship program with CPS Energy. They were looking for an infrastructure security analyst.

Pixley spent the summer of 2009 learning what being a cybersecurity analyst really meant. He participated in cleaning up systems, looking at intrusion detection system logs, and even starred in the company's first cybersecurity awareness video. At the end of his internship, he was offered temporary employment and was later hired on as a level one Infrastructure Security Analyst.

He spent four more years learning the inner workings of the company and was eventually promoted to become the manager of infrastructure security in the summer of 2014. All eyes were now on Pixley as the manager. He was responsible for an entire team and for enforcing the cybersecurity controls used to secure his company.

As a manager, he quickly learned that he could not get anything done alone. His peers needed to be in lockstep with everything he was trying to do. As a result, he spent the first two years of his management career building his team and relationships at CPS Energy.

He attributes much of his success to this collaborative effort. During those three years as a manager, he was able to bridge gaps between enterprise IT security and operational business units that had never existed before, getting security analysts invited to meetings at the beginning of a project instead of at the end. He even formulated the first ever cybersecurity governance committee, which provided senior chiefs with a quarterly briefing on all cybersecurity measures. He also created the first data security addendum to be used in the company's master services contracts.

After seven years, in the summer of 2017, CPS offered Pixley a position as director of threat intelligence and security awareness. This new but important department managed the gathering of cyber threat intelligence, understanding it, and disseminating it to business units for operational use. The department also created training programs, making users more aware of possible threats by creating scenarios for them to experience things like phishing emails or unauthorized thumb drives.

Within a year, Pixley was managing a fully mature cybersecurity awareness program that would later win the 2020 CSO 50 award for best cybersecurity awareness program. Pixley and his team implemented the first ever threat intelligence program and were able to establish relationships with federal, state, and local information sharing agencies.

During his three years as a director, Pixley also had the opportunity to be on the leadership team for the Large Public Power Council's cybersecurity taskforce. And to lead a team of cyber professionals who developed a white paper on cybersecurity operations centers for utilities.

He also started and completed his master's in business administration as well, at the University of Texas at San Antonio, in 2020. Then he attended and completed Harvard University's executive certificate program for "Cybersecurity: The Intersection of Policy and Technology." Pixley was also a guest lecturer at the University of Texas and the American Public Power Association's cybersecurity summit.

Pixley continues to work with people across his company, building relationships and understanding individual business unit requirements. That way, when someone does try to make a change, they understand where his team is coming from and Pixley understands what they are trying to achieve. Articulating customer constraints and their goals. This enables Pixley to organize his efforts to help them achieve their goals securely.

He attributes much of his success to the values he gained in the military. He learned hard work and discipline, how to make sure he got the job done. More importantly, he learned how to develop his communication skills and what he can offer his team.

To Pixley, the most rewarding part of his job is getting to serve the people that are in enterprise IT security and threat intelligence and security awareness, being a leader to help them accomplish their goals. Additionally, he feels good seeing his program grow and establishing a solid cybersecurity program through a support network of senior leadership.

Storms

Working as a lineman for the Gulf Coast Electric Cooperative, based in Wewahitchka on the Florida Panhandle, between Tallahassee and Panama City, wasn't going to be a walk in the park. U.S. Army veteran Frank Bailey had to be prepared and ready for action, for the many storms that go through the region.

During Hurricane Michael, in October of 2018, Gulf Coast Electric had around twenty-four thousand consumers out of power. When the storm hit, Bailey and his team had no idea what to expect. There were pine trees laying on top of our houses, sometimes with people still trapped inside.

But Bailey went to work, pulling sixteen to seventeen hours a day for two weeks before the Gulf Coast Electric crews started taking some breaks. From all over the southeast, mutual assistance crews of utilities in Louisiana,

Mississippi, North Carolina, Tennessee, and Texas came to help. Even with all of their efforts, the last customers to get power back had to wait until the twenty-third day after the outage had begun.

The hardest part for Bailey was working while his wife and two kids stayed at the house on a generator with nothing to eat. Most stores weren't open. And there was no gas to cook.

For Bailey, being a lineman is just like the military. He's been a lineman for Gulf Power Electric for nine years now – since completing his four years of active duty in 2012, as a CH-47D heavy lift helicopter door gunner – and he loves it. Not everyone is willing to join the military, let alone deployed to a combat zone as Bailey was. The same goes for building power lines. It's not easy work.

Also, a cooperative can have the same sort of brotherhood that Bailey experienced in the military. The linemen watch each other's back all day long out there.

SCADA in Alaska

After Brad Vander Plas left the U.S. Army, he later received a thirty-percent disability rating. Now, in addition to his monthly disability check from the Veterans Administration, he is also in the VA healthcare system. When he retires, he won't have to pay for health insurance.

And he qualified for vocational rehabilitation. So, while working at a Kinko's copy center and getting muscle spasms several times a day, he started the program. His counselor suggested he try taking some drafting courses to start off and then take a basic math refresher. Vander Plas realized that he really enjoyed drafting. He ended up getting a drafting certificate in 2003 and then his associates degree in 2004, both from the University of Alaska at Fairbanks.

While his wife was working, he had been stay-at-home dad to their kids while going to school. Now he was ready to switch places. He started working as a drafter for a precast concrete products company in Fairbanks, University Redi-Mix. He wasn't making a ton of money. But he liked the work.

He later saw that Alkan Shelters was advertising a position for a drafter designer. There, starting in the spring of 2004, he learned how to do three-dimensional modeling. The company was taking military shelters and redesigning them using carbon fiber and fiberglass. It was fun working in research and development. He still wasn't making a ton of money.

Then, one day his wife decided to see if they were hiring at Golden Valley Electric Association, the local cooperative utility. And they happened to be looking for a CAD and GIS technician. He put his resume together, applied, and was hired in the spring of 2009. Golden Valley Electric serves around a hundred thousand customers in the most populated interior area of Alaska, in Fairbanks, Delta Junction, Nenana, Healy, and Cantwell. Vander Plas ended up working in that role for about a year.

Towards the end of that first year, his supervisor had to leave the company. Vander Plas and two others applied to take over the position. Even though he was the newest of them, he got the job and stayed in the supervisor position for seven years, until the spring of 2016.

During his time as supervisor, Vander Plas worked with a lot of people throughout Golden Valley Electric. He got to know some of the system dispatchers and the dispatchers' managers. While working with them over the years, he realized he was not enjoying his own job very much. And he was also looking again to make more money.

When another dispatcher job position opened up, he talked to the manager, who explained what the job was like, but also that they were moving to twelve-hour shifts working every other week. More time off and more money. That was very attractive to him.

Vander Plas now works as a power systems dispatcher. He and his team are like the firemen of Golden Valley Electric. While there are always daily tasks to accomplish, most of the time they're simply monitoring or doing other important tasks. Then, suddenly something urgent happens. They're the ones that put it all back together, directing the traffic and making the decisions to get power back on.

Vander Plas confronts a lot of tough situations in Alaska as several large storms roll through regularly each winter. Many of these storms can last days on end. It can make work stressful to say the least.

Then, in the summertime, it's still busy as localized thunderstorms come through, causing wind to knock trees down into power lines or lightning to strike something nearby and cause an outage. Vander Plas also continues to be amazed at the number of suicidal squirrels in Alaska. The second-highest cause of outages is small animals or birds.

Even though he was injured, he believes being in the Army helped him tremendously. It instilled discipline in him, the ability to overcome adverse conditions, and to keep pushing forward. It gave him the confidence that whatever life threw at him, he could persevere and make it through.

Lieutenant to CEO

Jeff Ihnen began his career in the U.S. Navy in February of 1990 with formal training at Naval Station, Newport, Rhode Island. He then transferred to Crystal City in Arlington, Virginia to begin work at Naval Reactors. After a year into his tour at Naval Reactors, Ihnen went to the Bettis Atomic Power Laboratory, earning a master's in nuclear engineering in 1991. His specific expertise was in submarine fluid systems.

Post-Navy, he went on to earn a master's in mechanical engineering from the University of Wisconsin at Madison. That's where La Crosse, Wisconsin-based Michaels Energy recruited him from. The firm was just two years old at that point. That is where he is today, at this energy efficiency engineering consultancy, twenty-five years later.

After his first five years, Ihnen was promoted to energy division manager. Nine years after that he was promoted again to managing principal and two years later to vice president. Then, in January of 2016, Michaels made him its CEO. He has served in that capacity ever since.

Ihnen considers that while not all his Navy experience is relevant in his current position, a lot of it does apply. His current work has a heavy element of thermodynamics, heat transfer, and fluid dynamics. So, his studies in nuclear engineering school have bolstered his work. His company uses the interview tactics he took from his Naval experience to vet engineering candidates for strengths in thermodynamics, heat transfer, fluids, and other concepts.

What Ihnen has grown to love during his career, is continuing to learn more and more. In the utility industry, learning is practically endless. In the last few years, he has come to have a better understanding of the industry's supply side and the utility business model. He has focused more on how to keep rates low for customers and why that matters as well. He believes that finally, the demand side must be managed along with supply side resources to manage the grid and keep the lights on.

Pictured: Miranda Penn (top left), Iliana Rentz (top right), Cassandra Wheeler (center left), Jeff David Electric Cooperative rebuilding their system after Hurricane Delta (center right, photo courtesy of Chad Simon), Kelcey Brown (bottom, left)

Pictured: Kersha Brown (top), Stephanie Roper (center left, far right), Ming-wa Hui (center right), Sophia Eccleston (bottom)

Pictured: Iliana Rentz (top left), Monique Carter (top right, left), Sophia Eccleston (center), Ming-wa Hui (bottom left), Kelcey Brown (bottom right, right)

CHAPTER FIVE

Advice To and From Veterans

Lessons Learned, To Be Learned, To Unlearn

Traits

Consolidated Edison's DeAnne Ostrowski heartily believes that veteran applicants are a good source of professional talent for the utilities industry. Her reasons? Because vets, first of all, tend to be service-oriented. That's the way they were trained and that was their immersive experience in the military. Because vets, secondly, are inherently inclined to overcome obstacles, constantly looking for solutions. And, thirdly, because they're compliance, process and safety driven. All of these are core traits that the industry seeks.

Buzzwords

When asked what the utilities industry should do to attract veterans, Duke Energy's Sean Grier says companies should ensure that vets are in the mix. To do this, companies should actively search out vets they can include in the interview pools. And then see to it that they are seriously considered during the decision process.

It's especially critical if a veteran's resume does not contain certain buzzwords that recruiters prioritize. Many of these recruiters are using computer software these days to pick out resumes. The problem is this. Qualified applicants with atypical backgrounds such as vets can get thrown away because the software didn't detect a buzzword. So, the process can easily become exclusionary in unintentional ways.

Grier explains. A lot of veterans don't realize they need to tailor resumes according to each job application. Which can be common knowledge among competing applicants from the civilian world.

He thinks hiring managers need to tell recruiters to send all the resumes, not just the ones selected by the software or the recruiters themselves. In fact, that's what Grier does at Duke. When utilities fail to make that extra effort to look at veteran applicants, they miss out on a part—a potentially valuable part—of the overall talent pool.

The utilities industry, for example, generally screens for applicants with a grade point average of 3.0 or higher. Grier disagrees with that approach. Many of the people who work for him didn't average a 3.0. Though they are nevertheless exceptional engineers.

Many of those who come from the military don't have a 3.0. Because by the time a veteran gets to college, he or she is already an adult, perhaps with a family to consider as well. These individuals might be going to school full-time while working a part-time or even full-time job. In these circumstances, it might be particularly difficult to maintain a grade point average of 3.0 or above.

His advice for veterans entering the civilian workforce is to carefully consider working with utilities. The industry is a good place for them and offers a stable job. No matter how much financial, weather, or health disasters hit the country, everybody wants power. They're going to figure out a way to pay for it.

For the Long Haul

MidAmerican Energy's Kelcey Brown is a long-time member of the board of the organization, Veterans in Energy. It's not surprising she believes that the utilities industry is a place with considerable potential for veterans transitioning into the civilian workforce.

The industry is increasingly challenging itself to work harder at developing job descriptions that get veterans in the door in different types of roles. Not only as line workers, mechanics, or engineers. Brown and other industry leaders are convinced that vets can be brought into a variety of positions in cybersecurity, data analytics, accounting, and more.

Training in the military, admittedly, does not always translate seamlessly into a civilian career. But Brown also believes that the industry is working harder to give the veterans it hires ample opportunities for accelerated learning.

It's crucial that vets really learn about the utilities industry so they can later leverage the leadership experience that they gained in the military. This paves the way for vet employees to grow into a long-term utilities career.

Society is changing. People don't necessarily see themselves as sticking around for twenty-five or thirty years with the same company. Brown thinks that's another way in which vets bring so much value. They come into a company, learn the business, then develop with you. There is immeasurable value.

Instead of hiring and training new people, you get characteristic loyalty, commitment, and passion from retained vets.

Safe

First and foremost, the military focuses on safety. It is inculcated into everything you do in aviation, according to CPS Energy's Brook Bedell, who was an aviation planner in a war zone, or in the U.S. Army at large for that matter.

Similarly, utilities also put a premium on safety. Bedell has been all about safety since coming to work at CPS. This came quite naturally to him. As a twenty-year Army vet, he's attended safety briefings for as long as he can remember.

Additionally, there are a lot of overlapping themes between the utilities industry's core values and the military's core values. This is the case regardless of military branch. And there is a similar commitment—between the two worlds—to excellence, integrity, putting people first, and loyalty.

For Bedell, it was a great transition from the military to the utilities industry due to their sense of community. Both have as well the same sense of a good work ethic and ethos.

He explains that the transition from taking care of his soldiers was easy. In much the same way, Bedell's customers are his soldiers. He now takes care of them. In practice, this translates to the people who are served by CPS losing power from a service interruption. What can Bedell do at that moment to restore power as soon as possible to get his people back on track? Perhaps it's this sense of commitment and selfless service that leads former service members to gravitate toward the utilities industry.

So, what are Bedell's thoughts on how utilities can best attract, support, and retain other veterans? Most importantly, if you can't read the resume of a veteran applicant, he thinks they at least deserve a phone call from the company. Because these veterans have spent a decade or two submerged in military acronyms, abbreviations, and other things that the outside world has no idea about. In that phone call, the vet has the opportunity to verbally articulate or expand upon his or her experience that did not come through clearly within the resume.

Give Vets a Shot

American Water's Josh King offers some good advice to the senior leadership in the utilities industry. They should continue to lobby our government for more resources to help veterans, particularly for those vets returning from the most physically and mentally demanding environments. There are many homeless or traumatized veterans that need help. It's King's view that the nation needs to spend more money focusing on that kind of care for vets.

And companies in the utilities industry and other sectors as well really need to give veterans a shot. Even the ones that are struggling with things like chronic injuries and post-traumatic stress disorder can contribute a lot professionally.

Support

Georgia Power's Miranda Penn says that for utility companies to attract valuable veteran applicants, the companies need to connect with places like military bases and veterans' organizations. Furthermore, the companies need to stay in sync with those types of groups. If they do that, when vets exit military service, they will have immediate contacts to help them find their way, professionally, within the civilian world.

In Penn's opinion, it is not hard to hire veterans. In fact, it's very easy. Then, the question is, what is getting in the way? It is that many companies lack a deep understanding of the unique characteristics of the vets in their workforce.

Companies' leadership must understand that veterans are indeed unique. And that understanding of how the workforce can integrate and work well with them can have a big payoff.

Veteran employees may be struggling with post-traumatic stress disorder or emotional issues related to their military service. Penn believes it would even be helpful for leaders to receive some type of training themselves to help them navigate how to lead the vets in their workforce alongside the majority without military backgrounds.

Additionally, when someone leaves the military with all their valuable training and comes to work for a corporate company, the skill sets don't always transfer over seamlessly. It's especially difficult when companies don't consider military training to be valid work experience. If hiring companies ignore the wealth of training and leadership skills that veterans bring from the military, they completely miss out on a potential hire that could contribute great things to their team.

Penn's most important advice to young veterans is, if you're going to try to get a job with a big corporate company, be sure that this company not only hires veterans, but also supports them. Because hiring a veteran and supporting the veteran throughout their career is not the same exact thing.

She would advise them to make sure there are programs in place at these companies to give them support from the time they start to the time they leave that company. There must be ongoing support that meets your specific needs as a veteran. Otherwise, you may get lost and forgotten in the shuffle.

Hiring veterans needs to be much more than numbers. It's important to consider whether the company's veterans have gone on to be successful and what the company has done to facilitate and support that success.

Groups

American Water's Mike Rich's advice for the utilities industry's leadership is to have an avenue for conversations with the veterans in your organizations. Many companies, to their credit, are establishing employee resource or networking groups. Rich considers these a treasure trove for educating how to communicate with, gauge the morale of, retain, and engage veteran employees most effectively. Whenever veteran issues arise, these employee groups can address them and help advocate for those affected.

Through these groups, companies can reach out and talk to veterans and active-duty service members alike to get their feedback and make sure vets are adequately supported. In recent years, companies have changed the way they look at things like benefits or time off for National Guard and Reserve employees, so things are moving in the right direction.

Purpose

Tom Rollins believes that his company, Florida Power & Light, and other companies in the utilities industry offer a great opportunity for job-seeking veterans. But it's critical for vets to keep an open mind. Why is this so important? Because the industry's diversity of topics and of focus is incredibly broad. There are roles at the utilities across the state of Florida, for example, as linemen, truck drivers, and drone operators flying fixed-wing drones. And in administrative functions, at help desks, and in any number of other creative and innovative groups.

According to Rollins, private companies must not simply recognize but embrace the fact that, regardless of their past position or rank in the military, veteran applicants offer more to a position than just applying their technical skills. And why is this so important? Because larger private companies tend to target junior military officers with four to eight years of experience. This practice often leads to overlooking those vets with more than eight years of experience, which can relegate them to lower positions.

An applicant may be a veteran who has completed a four-year contract and nothing more. Another veteran may be an officer retiring after twenty years. In either situation and all those in between, these men and women often have more well-rounded and specifically tailored, specialized training than many other applicants from civilian backgrounds. And, they will always have in-depth leadership training as well.

Additionally, it's important for companies to focus on, not just identifying veterans' talents and making use of them, but learning how to truly engage them when they come in. In Rollins' opinion, if you want to retain a veteran, you need to convey a sense of purpose and positional impact within your company.

Rollins then elaborates. You can throw money at a veteran employee every year. You can give him or her retention bonuses or raises. But if the vets don't feel that they're making a difference in the company or the people around them, they're going to leave.

Mentor

Georgia Power's Cassandra Wheeler tirelessly advocates for a range of resources for helping veterans. Her goal is to help them reach their highest potential within the utilities industry. The organization she leads as its president, Veterans in Energy, and many other major organizations offer resources for helping veterans to transition into the civilian workforce, whether at utilities or elsewhere in the economy. Still, there are gaps where these or similar programs aren't easily accessible by vets.

She also believes that mentoring programs for veterans – formal or informal – are very beneficial. But Wheeler admits that no matter how much we are currently doing for vets, there are always other angles we haven't been able to make available or haven't yet thought up.

You're Not Alone

Rocky Mountain Power's Ron Wild offers this advice for veterans who have recently left military service. It is, very simply, that they should reach out. In other words, they don't have to go it alone. They don't have to start their civilian career without first developing and cultivating a network of potentially helpful relationships.

There are all kinds of assistance available through places like American Legion posts, Veterans of Foreign Wars, and other Veterans Affairs organizations. If a vet is wondering what they should do for the future, they should find other people to have conversations with, to gain a different insight, a different perspective.

Wild's advice for vets in the utilities industry is, additionally, to believe in yourself. And to never give up. He has advice for companies within the utilities industry as well. The best thing that they can do is tie in with local military bases or social action groups.

Whenever veterans have out-processing, utilities need to get a booklet right in front of each vet to show them that a new career in our industry could be awaiting them. If the companies aren't out there building a presence, creating relationships, they're just not going to have success hiring more vets. It's as simple as that.

Open Mind

Rocky Mountain Power's Noah Yarbrough feels that the utilities industry provides a way for veterans to showcase their talents, particularly their leadership skills. Whether it's performing tasks or getting reports in on time, or whatever else their company needs, a military member has likely faced something similar in their career.

The industry should know of the unique characteristics that most veterans share, Yarbrough believes. A vet serves for a bigger purpose, and so brings a lot to the table in that way. A vet is willing to go the extra mile. And a vet is dedicated to both their craft and to what they've been assigned to do.

Whatever values a vet has been taught in the service can transfer to the private sector and the utilities industry specifically. But military service and utility service have differences. Yarbrough recommends vets keep an open mind. They should fit in at the utility without sacrificing what they learned in the military. They should find a way to mix the two ways of working – military and civilian – and find a good balance between the two. Trying to learn as much as they can about the industry and a vet's civilian coworkers will serve them well in the long term.

Different Cultures

Some veterans, like ScottMadden's Kevin Hernandez, may have smooth transitions from military to civilian. However, for many it can be challenging even if they have skill sets that are directly relatable to civilian careers. It's very difficult to serve for ten, fifteen, or twenty years and be able to translate that experience into terms that are understandable by industry.

Hernandez notes that this is a key area for utility companies to be aware of when looking for talent. What can they do to ease those transitions? From a capability standpoint, translating someone's experience should be very easy.

For him, the transition was made easier by the similar cultures shared by the military and the power industry. The culture of the Navy translates well into nuclear power. When he went to work for a nuclear generator for a couple of years in Ontario, it almost felt like being back in the military. People were talking directly and in very similar terms. Procedures were written and followed a certain way. It was that kind of thinking that made it easy to relate to people in a new workplace culture. Even if you don't know the technical details, you're still having a similar conversation. You know where the holes are, what questions you need to be asking. It makes transitioning easier having that dialogue.

His transition was made easier by his role as a consultant as well. He describes consulting as still an intensive endeavor, with short time frames and high pressure. When he came to his firm, he was even warned by one of his senior partners, also a veteran, that communication was paramount. His partner explained that he would be working with a lot of people who were under pressure and that he might not feel it the same way they did due to his Navy experience. You still need to communicate with a client under pressure or with a stressed coworker. You recognize the issue and share the same sense of urgency.

To Hernandez, the important role companies can play in attracting and retaining veteran hires is centered on communication. The utilities industry and the military each speak their own language.

Even if you can take someone who has an electrical background in the military and put them in a position doing a similar function for utility, there are still those two different languages. This is what makes it difficult for both parties. It's hard for utilities to hire them because they don't know how to translate their job specifications. We need to learn who these veterans are, what they've been doing, and how those experiences are unique. Especially intangible qualities that are not directly relatable to a job description. We need to consider that they already have leadership training, that they're familiar with a high-stress environment and they can handle it. Not to mention they've worked with people from all different backgrounds and most have had multicultural experiences. Understanding these intrinsic values is crucial to truly understand what veterans bring to the table.

His advice to veterans considering the utilities industry is to highlight their communication and leadership skills. In the military, no day is the same, which is also true of the utilities industry. Everything is constantly changing, so if you like that fast-paced environment where the ground is always shifting a little bit, it's the perfect place.

Being A Lifeline

Florida Power & Light's Sophia Eccleston felt a true sense of pride during her military service. She was glad to serve the country that had taken her in, and she learned a lot about the military and its importance. More importantly, it fostered in her a renewed respect for veterans.

But when she returned stateside, she saw veterans on the street, homeless. Many would assume the worst of them, that in addition to PTSD, they might be alcoholics or drug addicts. Her response has always been that whether or not those assumptions are true, they were willing to die for American freedoms. We have a duty to help them because no matter what is going on with them right now, they were once willing to make the ultimate sacrifice for us.

Because of this, she developed a passion for combating homelessness. One of her missions in life continues to be helping the homeless, especially veterans, get off the street. She served as president of the Homeless Coalition of Palm Beach County for a couple of years and continues to serve on their board. She was also appointed by the Palm Beach County Board of Commissioners to serve on Palm Beach County's homeless advisory board.

She was later appointed by Governor DeSantis to serve on the CareerSource Florida Board, helping people find pathways into stable careers. During the COVID-19 pandemic, she was president of the board of the homeless coalition, and created a program called the Safe Shelter of Hope. This program provided hotels for homeless veterans and elderly living in parks, until they could find permanent housing or reunite with family.

Eccleston believes her company and the entire utilities industry is a great place for veterans to pursue a civilian career. Not just Florida Power & Light, but its parent company NextEra Energy, is very passionate about helping veterans and even focuses on recruiting veterans specifically. They also have an employee resource group called VetNext, made for veterans of NextEra to network within the company.

Her advice on what utilities can do for veterans is to be intentional about recruiting and hiring them. Focus on bringing veterans to the industry because they are disciplined. If you want a dedicated worker, somebody who's going to show up on time, who's going to get the job done, you hire a veteran. Being intentional about it is also a way of saying thank you to those veterans, who have given up their time, and left their families to serve this country.

Her advice for the veterans throughout our industry is to continue to maintain the brotherhood and sisterhood that they have. If you know a vet, if you know someone who is transitioning from the military that needs work, try to reach out to them. If you know a veteran that's looking for work, try to help them. Do whatever you can to help your fellow veterans because sometimes they don't necessarily know how to get into the industry.

And if you know someone who is struggling with the transition, try to do whatever you can to help. Not only can we help veterans get acclimated back into civilian life, but we can also help reduce veteran homelessness. Life happens to people, and not everyone handles the transition well. If we can help, we should help. You can't save everyone, but you must try.

Communication

Florida Power & Light's Iliana Rentz considered her transition from military to civilian an opportunity for growth. It was a new culture to explore and become familiar with. Things as simple as communication worked quite different.

In the military, you might assign a task and ask for a report when it's complete, all of which could be accomplished in practically a one-line email. In the civilian world, there are more formalities and professional niceties to observe. What she would normally say in four words, she was now writing paragraphs for. And that took time to both complete and get accustomed to. The little things make a big impact, particularly on how you're perceived. She didn't want to be perceived as too direct, stiff, or unapproachable.

There were also lessons along the transition on career development. In the military, you have a set career path. If you do well at your job and continue your training, progression usually happens naturally. It's a consistent and trustworthy process. But in the civilian world, you're in charge of your own destiny.

However, the value that a veteran hire brings to their position is still a huge factor. The leadership skills, the discipline, and other strengths learned in the military, can help veterans get ahead. It's really about how we communicate and collaborate, and almost relearning that to some extent.

Rentz believes that the utility industry is one of the best to go into after separating from the military. She encourages young veterans to take advantage of programs built to help with that transition. As a board member for Veterans in Energy, Rentz is currently working with the organization on an initiative to revamp a translator tool.

The tool was developed for service members that are separating, as well as companies that are looking to hire veterans. It breaks down military branches by occupational specialties, providing descriptions of skills and comparing experience to commensurate education as well. Job-seeking veterans or civilian hiring managers are then able to search using this tool to have a better idea of where these veteran applicants might naturally fit.

Understanding Each Other

For Xcel Energy's Ming-wa Hui, transitioning from the military to the civilian workforce changed his understanding of the culture of a business environment. For instance, in the military there's always a hierarchy. You follow the person that you report to for good or bad all the way through putting your life on the line. In the civilian world, just because you're called a manager doesn't mean everybody's going to follow you. You must convince people you are worth following, and they have a choice not to do what you tell them to.

But even then, it's all so similar. In the utilities, office workers function just the same as military officers doing planning, logistics, design, and more. And both the utility business and the military have a sense of stability compared to many private industries. Utilities will always be needed by our communities.

His advice for attracting, retaining, and supporting veterans in our industry is to increase understanding. A big part of assisting in transitions is understanding these recruits and their skill sets. We must go beyond their specialty or title because military training has so much more depth beyond title than in the civilian world.

Hui offers the example of a one-star general who was brought in to work with his team one year. The general had no background in transmission or substations, but he was a one-star retired general. Hui knew immediately that he would be invaluable when doing strategy and planning. Who out there would have more strategic training than a one-star general? He didn't need a subject matter expert, he had engineers for that.

Fostering Relationships

According to Georgia Power's Monique Carter, many transitioning veterans who come into the industry can feel like their past experience is not valued. Someone who was a leader in the military, may come into Southern Company as an administrative assistant. However, they have opportunities to exhibit those leadership skills in and outside of his or her job through things like employee resource groups.

Carter's advice for those individuals is to remember that Georgia Power, like many companies in the utilities, is a relationship company. It's important to begin developing those relationships with people intentionally. Consider talking to other veterans who may have recently made the transition or who are now a successful person in the company. These are the colleagues and mentors that might help someone's transition by sharing their experiences and advice.

Another way to develop relationships is to seek out leadership opportunities within employee resource groups or committees. That way people can see leadership abilities gained during military service in practice.

This is exactly what Carter did from day one at Georgia Power, and it has helped her to gain the respect of the leaders in the company throughout her career. When it comes time to think of people to place into different roles or on special projects, her name comes up because she has exhibited the necessary skills along the way. Leaders and colleagues alike come to her if they need to be connected to someone because she practically knows everybody.

Her vocal nature and relationship building skills have even earned her the nickname "The Mayor of 241" at Georgia Power Headquarters, located at 241 Ralph McGill. And even though it is a nickname, she takes that title with a heavy responsibility.

Carter's advice to company leaders looking to attract and retain veteran hires is to take the time to really understand that veterans are a special group of people. They have put their lives down for the country, left their families for varying amounts of time, and lived a very disciplined life. Respect what they accomplished during their time in the military, and don't take it for granted when they're transferring their skills into the corporate world.

When someone who was leading a large group of people in the military has trouble being accepted or respected as a leader in the corporate world, it can be incredibly frustrating. Should you have to always start from the bottom of a company and work your way up? Rather, there could be avenues for transitioning from a leadership position in the military to a leadership role in the company. Leadership development programs that already exist can be adjusted to fit the unique skills of veterans who are ready to contribute their work ethic and skills to the utilities.

Be Aggressive

When it comes to advice for the utility industry on hiring veterans, MidAmerican Energy's Milt Buker believes the utilities are stuck in their ways. In the last ten years, however, a lot has changed very quickly due to new developments in technology. In addition, many of the people who have done great work in the last decade are retiring, so a lot of knowledge is being lost.

Buker asserts that veterans have the potential to fill the gaps and rise to the challenge of increasing advancements. While it might be difficult to translate a person's military experience to how it may contribute to a utility position, he notes that we should keep close to mind the importance of the skills they bring to the job versus what can be taught. A typical military service member is used to having to learn quick. They're used to having to provide leadership skills. They're used to having to respond in stressful times. They're used to attention to detail, even in the midst of a hurry-up-and-wait type of environment. Veterans have an outstanding sense of duty and drive. Couple that with education and what the business can teach them, and Buker says you have the perfect employee for the utility industry.

He reflects that all utilities should get more aggressive about hiring veterans. The more programs available offering former military personnel the starting legwork for apprenticeships into the trade, the more we can interpret resumes correctly and offer more on-the-job trainings. It's a lot more difficult to teach somebody the leadership to drive, the sense of duty, and the attention to detail from the beginning. The military has already taught many individuals those essential skills, making it easier to teach those individuals how to do a specific business activity.

Index

About the Author

Steve Mitnick

Steve Mitnick is the executive editor of Public Utilities Fortnightly, the nearly hundred year old institution dedicated to serving as a platform for discussion about electric, natural gas, and water utility regulation and policy, in the public interest, and the principal owner of PUF's publisher, Lines Up, Inc., based in Arlington, Virginia. In this capacity, he writes, constantly actually, for PUF, the digital weekly This Half Fortnight and more recently books, as well as hosts and produces informative video programs for the industry.

Born in Brooklyn, New York in the summer of 1952, he came of age too late to mourn and resent the departure of the Dodgers but in time to embrace the Yankees of Mantle, Maris, Berra, and Ford. Prohibited from travelling to the Bronx, Yankee Stadium's borough, he attended scores of Mets games in the presumably safer borough of Queens, enabling him to see them transform from "can't anybody play this game" to their 1969 miracle. Now in Washington, D.C. he's come to love the Baby Shark song and the Nats as well.

Mitnick is an obsessive collector of artifacts and chronicler of utility history. Whether it's the strange journey of Reddy Kilowatt or the birth of the electricity industry in the late nineteenth century or the investor-owned versus public power fisticuffs of the nineteen thirties or the evolution of utility regulation throughout the twentieth century, Mitnick is researching and writing about the industry's stories seemingly without rest.

But most of all Mitnick is passionate about the people of the utilities industry, past, present, and future too. He loves highlighting and celebrating those that dedicate their careers to serving the public providing them with the essential elements of modern life safely, reliably, affordably, and cleanly.

About the Author

Rachel Moore

Rachel Moore is Senior Staff Writer of Public Utilities Fortnightly. In this role, she writes and edits content for PUF's publisher, Lines Up, Inc., based in Arlington, Virginia.

She is a proud Hokie, having graduated with her Bachelor of Arts in Literature and Language from Virginia Tech in 2018. She later received her Master of Fine Arts in Creative Writing from Queens University of Charlotte in 2021. Her previous work has been featured by The Tab, Philologia research journal, Avalon Literary Review, and several literary magazines. A chapbook of her poetry was published by Dancing Girl Press in 2019.

She is thrilled to be using her writing skills to promote and celebrate the innovations and innovators of the energy and utilities industry.